Men Really DO Listen:

How Men Listen Differently Than Women

FRANK FELSBURG

Foreword by Paul Haughton, PsyD

Publisher:

Cogent Training & Consulting

ISBN and Copyright Information

ISBN 978-0-9829976-3-5
Copyright © 2011

Cogent Training & Consulting
P O Box 852
Narberth, PA 19072
484-680-0962

www.cogenttraining.com
info@cogenttraining.com

Cover Design: Jack Camden

To my father

Table of Contents

Acknowledgments

In no particular order, here are a few acknowledgements: John Chomiczewski, for being a steadfast friend throughout the process; Michele (the "Yo" girl) Dash, for her encouragement; my Tuesday morning group (especially Steve Harrison, for leading the group—keeping Groucho Marx in mind); Geoffrey Berwind, for his brilliance (and his allowing me to use Bunbury); Karen McConlogue, for her candid remarks about my first draft; my editor Denise Crawford; Inscape Publishing; my sister Jeanne and her husband, Dempsey Butler; Stacy Boone; Kathy Snead; Rudy Tacconelli; Tim Tuinstra; Ms. Blum from Haverford High for caring; Debbie Watson; Jim Smith, Jr.; Betsy Noble; Dr. Bill Thompson; my colleagues at Magnum Group; all the men out there who have been accused of not listening and a slew of other people who encouraged me to keep going.

And, most importantly, my wife Pam, who listened to me talk about this book for a looong time.

Foreword

*If only you would **listen** to me.....*

This simple phrase has been at the core of communication difficulties since the dawn of time. Not only within the simple interactions of two people, but entire nations have struggled with people not understanding how to truly listen to each other with disastrous results. We often confuse the basic act of **hearing** someone—taking in their words—with the more complex, nuanced process of taking the time to **listen.** We overlook the fact that to truly listen is a skill involving verbal with nonverbal communication, tracking the flow of communication, listening for hidden meanings, and all the while placing the subject of what is being said within the broader context of the situation and perhaps the history of the two people. As a psychologist, for example, I am trained to focus not only on the **content** of what is being said, but also the entire **process** by which it is said.

It sounds complex, but it can be done! We all know of people who seem to do this naturally, who gaze at us in a focused manner, and we truly feel we are being heard and understood. We all can recall someone close that we have relied on, but we also marvel at people within businesses who can tune into our needs within an initial visit. Alas, for the rest of us we need some help (whether we realize it or not). Even when we may develop some listening skills within one context (i.e., the psychologist listening to a client in a session), we may still struggle with listening/communicating outside this context (the same psychologist trying to buy a car). I have found that some awful listening occurs at a party with just psychologists (or lawyers or doctors, etc.) We need a simple understanding of listening that is transferable across settings, across people. Skills that would help someone learn to listen for depth (deeper, emotional messages) as well as for basic messages (the bottom line).

And so along comes *Men Really DO Listen* by FJ Felsburg. Instead of a wordy treatise by a so-called 'expert' or a superficial 'self-help' book that sounds great but is readily forgotten, the book represents a journey to pull diverse elements together to gain a practical understanding—to begin to bridge the gaps that have occurred across groups (i.e., men vs. women) and professions in regards to listening. It is an honest journey, as I know Frank discovered the need for such a book through his own experiences. People kept saying that they weren't being listened to, and so Felsburg went to work to explore why— gathering information by carefully *listening* to others with no set theory or agenda. (I know very well as he elaborately interviewed me). The result is admirable—a practical guide to help us all understand this crucial process. To all those who have been told "If only you would listen to me..." the book is a must.

-Paul Haughton, PsyD

Introduction

Let me just say right off the bat that I'm no Deborah Tannen. She has a PhD and I don't. I don't even have a masters degree. On top of that, I didn't get married until I was 47 years old. So I'm certainly no relationship expert.

So why am I writing this book, and why should you read it?

While Tannen is an expert on linguistics and conversational styles, my focus is on the listening aspect of communication. Quite frankly the topic of listening intrigues me. I have given hundreds of seminars and presentations on it. And personally, I consider myself a fairly good listener. Not nearly as good as many other people, but better than many. And I'm a man. Imagine that.

Some people say to me, "If you're such an expert on listening, then why haven't I heard of you?" The reply is simple: "You weren't listening," I say facetiously.

My experience has been that listening takes time. The busier we are, the more things slip through the cracks. I know that while I've been extremely busy at times, I've tried to live a balanced life and not burn the candle at both ends. I realize this is easier said than done. However, as a result of this less-than-frenetic lifestyle, I can remember some things better than other people can. In fact, I can vividly remember things that happened thirty years ago, yet often I can't remember what I had for lunch yesterday.

John Gray said in his book *Men Are from Mars, Women Are from Venus* that his wife often accused him of not listening to her. The reality is, as a psychologist, he'd be listening to people all day long at work. He'd come home and want to relax. The reason was that he wasn't in a listening frame of mind. He was tired, and he had other things on his mind. As a result of this exhortation from his wife (and that's usually what it is when a woman says a man isn't listening), he decided to see two fewer clients and "schedule" her as his last appointment of the day. Things got much better after that.

To some people, this may seem cold. Yet it was very successful.

My friend Martin is a happily married businessman in his 40s. He knows when he's going to be listening to his wife, Tina, talk, she's going to be doing most of the talking. Which means his mind will have a tendency to wander, and, as a result, he'll be battling fatigue. If he shows Tina the slightest indication he's not listening, she will be extremely offended. So he combats this by finding the most uncomfortable chair in the house to sit in while she vents her feelings. This prevents him from drifting off into never-never-land and apparently works for him.

This anecdote shows that men are trying. Many other stories like this show that the stereotype that men don't listen doesn't ring true. Or at least we don't hear it.

This book has taken a long time to come to fruition. The idea for it was planted when I told a woman I know that I'd like to write a book on the topic of listening. She said to me, "What does a man know about listening?" Here's my answer.

Section One

Where We Are

In this section, I start with some general information where I talk about the benefits of listening. I then get into the potentially provocative area of gender differences. Exploring further, I next address linguistics and dialects. I've also included some humorous anecdotes near the end of the section.

"I remind myself every morning. Nothing I say this day will teach me anything. So if I'm going to learn, I must do it by listening." – Larry King

Chapter One

The Importance of Listening

Good communication is hard work. It may look (and even feel) effortless, but is sometimes anything but. We may think we're communicating effectively, but often we aren't.

Crystal clear communication is essential in many situations. Consider a safety director conveying information to fellow employees, a nurse telling a doctor about a patient's medical condition or an air traffic controller helping a pilot land his plane.

In relationships, particularly marriage, communication is probably the most important thing. However, with the busyness in our lives, many conversations between spouses sound like the old Abbott and Costello routine "Who's on First?" The truth is that some problems in communication arise because of the partners' different speaking styles, which include timing, pacing, pausing and loudness.

Men Really DO Listen

The Cornerstone of Communication

Listening is the cornerstone of communication. Of the four main communication methods (speaking, reading, writing and listening), listening is the one we use the most. It is estimated that on average we spend about 40 percent of our time listening, 35 percent speaking, 16 percent reading and 9 percent writing. Going through our educational school system, we're taught how to read, write and speak; but rarely are we ever taught how to listen. Interestingly enough, the task that's focused on the most, writing, is the one we use the least. The one we use the most, listening, isn't even taught!

Listening is a lost art. Most people listen at only about 25 percent efficiency. Many people think the opposite of talking is waiting to talk. Yogi Berra said you can observe a lot by watching. I say you can learn a lot by listening.

According to International Listening Association member John Stewart (not to be confused with from two Anglo-Saxon words. One word is *hlystan*, which means "hearing." The other is *hlosnian*, which means "to wait in suspense." Listening, then, is the combination of hearing what the other person says and a suspenseful waiting, an intense psychological involvement with the other person.

With all the distractions these days, listening is more of a challenge than ever. Even public libraries, where I conducted much of the research and did some of the writing of this book, are

The Importance of Listening

extremely noisy, with loud conversations, cell phones, tutoring and babies crying. Organizations advertise and talk about how great they are at listening, yet they often don't walk their talk.

A Good Habit to Develop

Habit number five in Stephen Covey's book *The Seven Habits of Highly Effective People* is "Seek first to understand, then to be understood." About this habit, he says, "The only basis where someone is open to influence is when they feel they've been understood." Having an increased awareness of listening and knowing how to do it more effectively can help salespeople, spouses, coworkers and neighbors. Truly listening to someone is almost like reading their mind. Or, as many women feel, really listening to someone is the same as being loved.

M. Scott Peck in *The Road Less Traveled* says, "Listening well is an exercise of attention and by necessity hard work. It is because they do not realize this or because they are not willing to do the work that most people do not listen well." Peck says great listening requires total concentration: "You cannot truly listen to anyone and do anything else at the same time." He later says, "Since true listening is love in action, nowhere is it more appropriate than in marriage. Yet most couples never truly listen to each other."

Listening takes patience, time and humility, all of which seem to be in rather short supply these days. Countries and couples need to listen to and respect each other. The simple act of doing so could prevent wars and disagreements from taking place. Parents need to listen to their children, and children need to listen to their parents. If everyone talks at the same time, then no one is listening. Many people think listening puts one in a subservient position. They're afraid to give up control. Yet giving up that control is what many people need to do. Growing up, I often subscribed to the motto "It's better to remain silent and be thought a fool than to open one's mouth and remove all doubt." Just because someone doesn't say much doesn't mean they're a good listener, but keeping your mouth shut is a start.

Listening helps because we live in such a busy world, and we often want to be heard. We want to feel that our opinion matters. For that reason, the gift of listening can be of tremendous benefit to someone's self-esteem. Swiss psychiatrist Dr. Paul Tournier once said, "It is impossible to overemphasize the immense needs humans have to be really listened to, to be taken seriously, to be understood."

Good listening even affects your health. The book *Emotional Intelligence* by Daniel Goleman says, "Finally, there is the added medical value of an empathic physician or nurse, attuned to patients, able to listen and be heard. This means fostering 'relationship-centered care,' recognizing that the relationship between physician and patient is itself a factor of significance. Such relationships would be fostered more readily if medical education included some basic tools of emotional intelligence, especially self-awareness and the arts of empathy and listening."

Historically, public figures known to have been good listeners include not only Jacqueline Kennedy and Mother Teresa, but also Calvin Coolidge (aka Silent Cal), Henry Fonda, Joe DiMaggio and Bill Clinton. Barack Obama jokes about the size of his ears, but history will judge whether he was a good listener or not.

When we're tired, it's harder to listen. Our thoughts tend to drift. This often happens when women speak because they focus on details and men want facts.

Listening pays off in many ways other than in conversation. Here are a few examples:

Speeches: Some of us are moved by eloquence. Rev. Dr. Martin Luther King, Jr.'s *I Have a Dream* speech is a thing of beauty. Many of us have been moved to make career decisions based on what we heard someone say. Obama's campaign speeches, FDR's fireside chats and JFK's oratory all have inspired millions.

Music: Music (both classical and contemporary) has had an incredible impact on our lives as humans. In fact, the way we differ from other mammals is by listening. Russian composer Igor Stravinsky was known to have said, "To listen is an effort, and just to hear is no merit. A duck hears also."

Men Really DO Listen

Poetry: For centuries, poets have been using words to evoke emotion from readers and listeners alike. Alfred Lord Tennyson, Robert Frost and Dylan Thomas have all brought tears to the eyes of listeners and readers of their poems. They use devices that encourage us to use all of our senses to experience their feelings, ideas or concepts. Some of these devices include imagery, alliteration (repeating the same sound in consecutive words like "Adam's apple," "baby blue" or "March madness") and rhyme. Onomatopoeia, a word that imitates the sound it represents (for example "hiss," "buzz" and "bark"), is also used for dramatic effect.

Sounds of Nature: Birds chirping, frogs croaking, and thunder are sounds that many of us hear on a regular basis. Other sounds of nature that are not as common for most of us, but that do exist for many include lions roaring, horses neighing and seals barking.

Crowds of People: The roar of a crowd at a sporting event can be a wonderful thing, often depending on which team a spectator is rooting for.

Consider what Mother Teresa said about listening: "Before you speak, it is necessary for you to listen, for God speaks in the silence of the heart." I know people whose lives turned completely around while they listened to a musical recording or to prophetic words.

The Importance of Listening

In addition to all the positive effects of listening, consider the negative effects of *not* listening. The most overt example is that when people feel others are not listening to them, they sometimes resort to violence. This was evident in the school shootings in Littleton, Colorado; Lancaster, Pennsylvania; and at Virginia Tech. As a byproduct of doing research for this book, I discovered that one of the biggest insults you can give someone, particularly a woman, is not to listen to them. What would happen if no one listened? Great ideas wouldn't get acted on. Have you ever stopped to think about all the wonderful thoughts that didn't come to fruition because they fell on deaf ears?

Conclusion

If a tree falls in the woods and no one is around to hear it, does it make a sound? People have debated this philosophical question for years. We now know that, yes, acoustically it does make a sound, but communication needs a sender and a receiver. The tree example has no receiver in the equation. So we might say that in this instance it *doesn't* make a sound. Perhaps you have heard the spoof of this question, that goes something like "If a man speaks in a forest, and no woman is around to hear him, is he still wrong?" Obviously, that's cynical. Nevertheless, I will discuss these and other misnomers and myths in the chapters that follow.

This book is about communication and the challenges that go with it. In the chapters that follow, I'll attempt to illustrate the ways we speak

Men Really DO Listen

and listen and how—even when done effectively, if they're done in the wrong environment—they can wreak havoc and cause miscommunication and heartbreak.

"Shut up and kiss me." –Mary Chapin Carpenter

Chapter Two

Gender Differences

I was playing basketball with a bunch of guys, and someone asked the question, "Why are babysitters always girls?" And someone astutely replied, "Because boys have an external organ, and girls have an internal organ." "What does that have to do with anything?" I initially thought. Then I thought, "That's interesting." And that does explain a lot: like why men are often aggressors and women often victims, why men (almost) always come on to women and why men are less sensitive than women. As Abraham Maslow said, "When the only tool you have is a hammer, you look at everything as a nail."

Men are accused of thinking with the wrong part of their body. This often gets them into trouble. But, besides the obvious physical differences between men and women, other differences exist, particularly behavioral. For example, men's egos often get in the way, preventing them from understanding certain situations. I'll enumerate some of the other differences later in this chapter.

Men Really DO Listen

You might say these differences are a combination of nature and nurture. Therefore, the way we were brought up makes a big difference.

It All Starts When We're Young
CHILDHOOD

Dr. Deborah Tannen, author of *You Just Don't Understand,* (a New York Times bestseller for nearly four years) as well as Daniel Maltz and Ruth Borker studied boys and girls growing up. From her observations, Tannen reports that the challenges of male-female communication are basically cross-cultural, even if both grew up in the same household. The reason men and women often have trouble communicating, she concludes, is because they grew up in different worlds. Boys and girls are treated differently, so not surprisingly, they act and communicate differently. Their research indicated that, for the most part, boys didn't play with girls. My experience has been that, in general, boys don't particularly care for girls, at least not until they approach adolescence and puberty.

In the book *Emotional Intelligence*, author Daniel Goleman references work done by John Gottman and J. Parker and says, "One study of children's friendships found that three-year-olds say about half their friends are of the opposite sex; for five-year-olds it's about 20 percent, and by age seven almost no boys or girls say they have a best friend of the opposite sex."

Gender Differences

The differences between boys and girls eventually translate into differences between men and women.

Girls' Worlds

In a major study of gender differences, sociologist Janet Lever observed that in the play of school-age children, girls play indoors more than boys. They play house, dress up or with dolls. Girls' worlds are not as competitive as boys' worlds. Girls' lives are more about cooperation than competition. Their games don't necessarily have a winner and a loser, as boys' games do. Girls often have a best friend and play in smaller (more intimate) groups.

Girls develop a more proficient use of language than boys. Maltz and Borker say that "basically girls learn to do three things with words: 1) to create and maintain relationships of closeness and equality, 2) to criticize others in acceptable ways, and 3) to interpret accurately the speech of other girls." Maltz and Borker also say that "to a large extent friendships among girls are formed through talk. Girls need to learn to give support, to recognize the speech rights of others, to let others speak, and to acknowledge what they say in order to establish and maintain relationships of equality and closeness." And, they don't like to rock the boat or boast about their athletic ability.

For girls, talk is the glue that holds relationships together.

Men Really DO Listen

Boys' Worlds
Boys' relationships are held together primarily by activities: doing things together or talking about activities such as sports or, later, politics.

The boys groups are larger and include a wider age range. Boys often have a leader who says, "Do this" and "Do that." Girls would consider this behavior "bossy." Leaders of boys' groups are often those with the most athletic prowess or the one who is boldest.

Also, boys' games last longer. In the United States, people have a competitive mentality in which you play until someone wins. In American football, for instance, it's called "sudden death." In Japan, however, things are different. There, it's more about the team than the individual. A book about Japanese baseball entitled *You Gotta Have Wa*, by Robert Whiting, brilliantly illustrates this. *Wa* is team spirit or harmony. In Japan, the ideal scenario is when the game ends in a tie. Everyone saves face and goes home. In America, a tie (for example, in ice hockey), is akin to "kissing your sister."

In one of Tannen's experiments of four different age groups, boys and girls were put in a room and told to talk to each other. Boys looked around the room and talked about objects in the room, whereas girls looked at each other and spoke more intimately. The boys' talk was more abstract. The boys "conversations" bounced all over the place, one of which was fifty-eight different subjects. The girls mostly introduced a subject, then dissected it.

ADOLESCENCE
Adolescent girls
A sixteen-year-old girl (who happened to be a tomboy and therefore more competitive than other girls her age) was asked if boys and girls talk differently. She said they both talk about their problems but girls go on and on. With boys, a boy brings up a problem, one of them solves it and they stop talking about it. Boys often talk to each other about troubles, but the other boy often downplays its significance.

Adolescent girls' lives are mostly about relationships. They read magazines like *People* and watch television shows like *Hannah Montana*. Girls do play in some predominantly male games, but rarely is the reverse true. These days (Tannen et. al's research was primarily done prior to the mid-1980s) girls are becoming more competitive, particularly in sports like soccer, tennis, golf, swimming, lacrosse and running.

Things are difficult for the popular girls. Because girls like to stay in smaller groups than boys, girls are not as comfortable in large groups. Everyone wants to be friends with the popular girls—the cheerleaders and the good looking ones. But they can't be friends with everybody. That goes against their nature. They have to be careful whom they associate with. As a result, they are often branded as "stuck up." If girls want to show they're friends with a popular girl, all they have to do is start telling others her secrets. That proves they are close to her, but they'll lose her as a friend if they do so.

Adolescent boys
In the tenth grade boys Tannen observed, they sat parallel to, rather than facing, each other, and their conversation proceeded on parallel tracks. The two boys simultaneously discussed two main topics, one of concern to each of them, whereas the girls at grades six and ten focused on the troubles of one of them.

When I was growing up, the leader was often the biggest wise guy in the group or in the neighborhood. He was unafraid of others and often irreverent. Maybe it was me, and that's just who I gravitated toward, but these leaders, with their devil-may-care attitude were the cool cats. I deified them.

My sister, on the other hand, who was close to me in age, smartly stayed away from these groups. She would play in her own more sedentary groups, instead of following me in the roving boys' groups. She was meeker. I was bolder.

My sister rebelled in her own way but turned out to be more stable emotionally, especially in early adulthood. Frankly, I took longer to mature. As the saying goes, "You're only young once, but you can be immature forever."

Gender Differences

ADULTHOOD
Women
The careers that women find themselves in are myriad. Many women today are the breadwinners in the household. While, as of the date of the printing of this book, a woman has not yet been president of the United States, women have broken through the glass ceiling and have held such distinguished positions as governor, secretary of state and speaker of the House.

Not that many years ago, women were typically depicted in ads as ditzy, especially blondes. To a large extent, that's changed. Partly as a result of the 1964 Civil Rights Act, along with a 1971 FCC ruling mandating equal employment regardless of gender, more women now work in places like newsrooms. These events, fueled by the feminist movement, led to increased opportunities— although not enough.

For the most part, women like to dance more than men (although men like to dance in the end zone when their football team scores a touchdown). Women want romance, men want sex. Women want to be wined and dined. Men generally go along with that only because that's what women want (Freud went to his grave wondering what women want).

Men
Men generally have bigger egos. Many were brought up to think they could do anything they wanted. They could conquer the world. In many ways, this conquering mentality could be part of

why conflict often occurs between men and women.

Men are often physically stronger than women because of the way their bones and muscles are structured. Therefore, they often find themselves cast in more strenuous jobs than women.

These Days

Regarding how things are different today than they were in the 1980s, Mary Pipher, author of *Reviving Ophelia* (written in the '90s), says, "The peer culture is much tougher now than when I was a girl. Chemicals are more available and more widely utilized. Teenagers drink earlier and more heavily. A speaker in my college class told about his life in a small Nebraska town in the early sixties. He said that in high school his buddies would buy a six-pack and cruise on a Saturday night after they dropped off their dates. After his talk a young woman in the class said that she lived in his hometown in the 1990s. He asked how it was different. She said, 'Kids buy cases, not six-packs, and the girls get drunk, too.'" That was over a decade ago. Imagine what things are like today.

In *Emotional Intelligence,* Goleman says about girls today "antisocial teenage girls don't get violent—they get pregnant."

R-E-S-P-E-C-T

The gender lines are blurred now. Previously women weren't as interested in respect as men. Now, they seem to be. Our world is becoming more androgynous. Women are being taken seriously and are not seen so much as sex symbols anymore. Women are doing things only men did before, and that should be respected. Women are enlisting in and fighting in the armed forces. As a result, women now know what men have gone through. I think they have a greater appreciation for what men put up with and vice versa.

Alluding to the book *Handbook of Emotions* (New York: Guilford Press, 1993), and specifically in a review entitled "Gender and Emotion" by Leslie R. Brody and Judith A. Hall, Goleman says "Evidence for these different stances (between men and women) is very strong in the scientific literature. Hundreds of studies have found, for example, that on average women are more empathetic than men, at least as measured by the ability to read someone else's unstated feelings from facial expression, tone of voice, and other nonverbal cues. Likewise, it is generally easier to read feelings from a woman's face than a man's; while there is no difference in facial expressiveness among very young boys and girls, as they go through the elementary-school grades boys become less expressive, girls more so. This may partly reflect another key difference: women, on average, experience the entire range of emotions with greater intensity and more volatility than men—in this sense, women *are* more 'emotional' than men."

For example, Goleman says in the chapter "Intimate Enemies," "When girls play together, they do so in small intimate groups.... One key difference can be seen when games boys or girls are playing get disrupted by someone getting hurt. If a boy who has gotten hurt gets upset, he is expected to get out of the way and stop crying so the game can go on. If the same happens among a group of girls who are playing, the *game stops* while everyone gathers around to help the girl who is crying. This difference between boys and girls at play epitomizes what Harvard's Carol Gilligan points to as a key disparity between the sexes: boys take pride in a lone, tough minded independence and autonomy, while girls see themselves as part of a web of connectedness. Thus boys are threatened by anything that might challenge their independence, while girls are more threatened by the rupture in their relationships."

I haven't played football in a long time, so I've forgotten some things like injuries. I must admit, when I'm watching a professional game of American football on television and someone gets hurt, I don't empathize with the injured player as much as my wife does. The player gets removed from the field, and I mostly forget about him unless I'm watching the game with my wife. She asks all kinds of questions about the injured player and, because she's a physician, often speculates as to what the injury might be. My mind is back on the game, and hers is there with the player as he gets an MRI. I tell myself I'm going to find out what happened to the player the next day, but, unless he's the hometown team's player—and a stellar one too—the newspaper often doesn't report the extent of the injury.

Gender Differences

Summary

The differences between men and women come down to both nature and nurture. Regarding nature, we're simply made differently by our creator. As for nurture, the reality is, boys and girls grow up differently. Also, our society has different expectations for women than for men.

Linguist Robin Lakoff postulated that boys and girls in contemporary America learn different ways of speaking by the age of five years or earlier. When these boys and girls grow up to be men and women, they see the world differently and, as a result, communicate differently. I'll focus on this topic in the next chapter.

"England and America are two countries divided by a common language." – George Bernard Shaw

Chapter Three

Linguistics

Linguistics is not an Italian pasta dish; it's the study of language. In particular, the study of individual and cultural distinctions regarding language is called anthropological linguistics.

If you stop and listen to the way we each speak, you'll notice each person has a distinct pattern to his or her speech. We pause differently. We use different pacing. We speak at different rates. Much of this has to do with how and where we were brought up. We frame things in a certain way. We are at times direct and at other times indirect.

In Deborah Tannen's book *That's Not What I Meant: How Conversational Style Makes or Breaks Relationships*, she discusses these nuances. She astutely points out that it's not what you say but how you say it that counts. Success depends on conversational signals like voice level, pitch and intonation, rhythm and timing, and simple turns of phrase.

Men Really DO Listen

People have different ways of speaking, depending on where and how they were brought up. Some men are the strong, silent type. Some women (as well as men) think they should speak only when spoken to. Other people are uncomfortable with silence. Some people are taught that children should be seen and not heard. Still others are told, "The squeaky wheel gets the grease." Many believe it never hurts to ask, as the worst someone can say is "no." And some believe (or are taught) that "you should never ask a question you don't know the answer to."

No study of linguistics (or gender for that matter) would be complete without introducing some of the concepts Tannen raised in her work. This chapter touches on some of these concepts (as well as others), since I believe nature and nurture affect the way we communicate.

Accentuate the Positive
Some people have accents. I don't. Never did. Never will. That's what we all think. Accents are not as distinctive, however, as they were before the advent of television. It's harder to tell where people are from now, because they don't have a distinguishing accent. But different regions do use different words. People in the Midwest (and Pittsburgh, surprisingly enough, is in the Midwest to most people on the East Coast) put their groceries in a sack or a saaaaack. They drink pop (not soda). Some people, especially those from the South, have a tendency to speak slower than "y'all from the Noth" (rhymes with both). Youse (a Philadelphia colloquialism) from the South are

Linguistics

never in a hurry to do anything, especially get your point across. People from the South use words like *reckon* and *dang* and use the word *cotton* as a verb. As in "We don't cotton to strangers around here." Y'all "might ought" to listen to yourselves sometimes.

My father told me he heard a guest on a radio program years ago, who could tell where a person calling in was from, right down to the county. This occurred before television and commercial air travel, which evened accents out quite a bit.

While many people are familiar with the work of Deborah Tannen, fewer are familiar with John McWhorter of The Manhattan Institute. McWhorter, an associate professor at the University of California, Berkeley, has written a number of books, among which are *The Power of Babel: A Natural History of Language; Losing the Race: Self-Sabotage of Black America* and *Doing Our Own Thing: The Degradation of Language and Music and Why We Should, Like, Care.* In *The Power of Babel*, McWhorter says the following about dialects:

> Language evolves not into just one language but several. This happens when speakers of a language move to different locations. In each place, different change pathways happen to be taken, each setting the scene for new changes in their turn, such that, through time, the various transformations of the original language are no longer mutually intelligible.

Men Really DO Listen

A person's past also affects how they perceive the world. It affects the way they talk, the way they think and who they relate to. It affects their speech. Many of us say what we feel. This verbal permissiveness is becoming more and more the case in our society. People who create television and movie humor are always pushing the envelope. Impressionable children and young adults often learn their vocabulary from popular television shows and movies. Now all kinds of words that used to be considered off limits are part of the vernacular. I call it soft-core cursing. Many people believe if it got by the television censors, then it's okay to use in public.

Desire

We all have different levels of passion for communicating. I am sometimes amazed at the lack of communication skills of employees on the front lines of customer interactions. Once I was in an office supply store where the clerk who rang up my order was barely speaking coherently. I was returning something, and the interaction did not go smoothly. After much difficulty, we consummated the transaction. As I was gathering up my receipts, two more customers went to this woman to have their purchases rung up. The surly clerk muttered something to each of them, but both of them asked her to repeat herself. This obviously did not help her attitude toward the task of communicating with the store's customers.

As previously addressed, sometimes we're just not in the mood to communicate. I don't know if the clerk's problem was apathy (which no one really cares about anymore anyway), or if it was a deficiency in her communication skills, but I DO know that at times I just don't want to talk.

Introverts and Extroverts
Some people are inhibited when they speak, even cautious—possibly because they said the wrong thing once. They're "snake bit," afraid to share their view of the world. They are afraid of being judged wrongly. Introverts want to keep to themselves. Many of them have learned to act like extroverts because "if you're going to get anywhere in this world, you have to learn to speak up."

Introverts are often better writers than extroverts. They often desperately want to communicate, but the spoken words (or how they present them) get in the way. Experts believe that people are born as one or the other. When people are tentative about expressing themselves verbally (as introverts often are), they tend to weigh every word so as not to offend. This often gets construed as indirectness or, ultimately, dishonesty.

Some children are often uninhibited. Until they reach puberty, they're rarely concerned with the consequences of what they say. After they reach puberty, they sweat under their arms and their hands get clammy when they have to say something important. A public speaking class for adolescents can be devastating.

Men Really DO Listen

Some people (like Greta Garbo) prefer to be alone, whereas others are more gregarious and want to be among others. Their identity is linked to those they associate with. They need a buffer, someone who, regardless of what they say, still loves them. Many people are like this. Having a close friend along gives them the courage to go out among other people.

Public Speaking

Public speaking is mostly about confidence. If you're an extrovert, you'll probably have little difficulty speaking in public. If you're an introvert or not a confident person, preparation is the key. Roger Ailes, in his book *You Are the Message*, said one should adhere to five basic things when speaking in public. First, you should be prepared. That's the Boy Scout's motto. Secondly, you should be able to make the audience feel comfortable. Third, you should be committed. Fourth, you should be interesting. And fifth, you should be likeable. He talks a lot about energy being important too.

Another important aspect of public speaking is intonation, which includes pacing, pausing, pitch and loudness. However, as Harvey Mackay said, "Don't mistake a loud voice for charisma." I had a friend when I was growing up that could make anything sound interesting by talking enthusiastically. He would say things with excitement. We've all heard people who could make reading the phone book sound interesting.

Linguistics

Conversation

Conversational devices include expressive reaction, asking questions, complaining and apologizing. Some people are tremendous conversationalists, and others work very hard at it. What follows are some of the concepts Tannen discusses in her books regarding conversation—and what may happen consciously or subconsciously—when they take place.

METAMESSAGES
Tannen talks a lot about metamessages: the message below the surface. They are often more powerful and more apparent than the surface or main message, especially to women. *Meta* means "beyond," as in metaphysics—beyond physics. Meta tags on a Web site are words or tags below the surface, behind the scenes. Metamessages are messages underneath or beyond the apparent message.

When I was young, my father used to insist that I wear a hat whenever I went outside in cold weather. The message was that he cared about me, but the metamessage was that I couldn't take care of myself. As Tannen says, "Information conveyed by the meanings of words is the message. What is communicated about relationships—attitudes toward each other, the occasion, and what we are saying—is the metamessage. And metamessages are what we react to most strongly. If someone says "I'm not angry," and his jaw is set hard and his words seem to be squeezed out in a hiss, you'll believe the metamessage conveyed by the way he said it.

Men Really DO Listen

"Why did you say it like that?" or "Obviously it's not nothing—something's wrong" are responses to metamessages of talk.'

DIRECTNESS VS. INDIRECTNESS

Once while attending a barbeque, I came in on the tail end of a conversation the host was having with another of his guests. She was telling him about how she had gotten sick on a trip she had just taken. She was still not feeling well, so was not going to eat any of the food that was cooking on the barbeque. I walked up and said, "Hi Sally, how are you?" She immediately responded, "Hi Frank, I'm fine. How are you?" Had we known each other better, she might have told me exactly how she felt. But because we were just acquaintances, she opted for the standard "I'm fine. How are you?" We don't mean the question literally. Yet we ask it all the time. It's part of our linguistics as a society. Had she responded with the truth, "I have diarrhea," I don't know that I would have known what to say. (Actually it might have made for a more interesting conversation had she told me the truth. Who knows?)

Some people are flat out direct. Others beat around the bush. In this country directness is associated with honesty (although I've heard it said, "Honesty is the best policy, but insanity is a better defense.") My sister happens to be very direct. I, on the other hand, sometimes have a hard time saying what I'd like to say. I once introduced my sister to a woman friend of mine who has three children, two with the same life-threatening illness. My sister asked her if they

Linguistics

had thought about not having additional children after the first was diagnosed, knowing that it was likely that subsequent children would also have the disease. I could and would never in a million years have asked such a hard question. To me it seemed almost rude. Yet my sister, being more direct than me, has little difficulty saying what's on her mind. I remember after she joined the Navy, she and a friend of hers subscribed to the philosophy that "we'll probably never see this person again." That allows you to ask questions you might otherwise never ask.

I normally try to be diplomatic when I speak. I like to build camaraderie. As a result, I rarely deal with an issue head on. As an introvert, I like to mull it over and come up with the best possible answer. My feeling is that, although an extrovert's way of dealing with a problem or issue may be seen as more honest or forthright, the introvert's answer or remedy is often more thorough and thoughtful.

I'm sure you've heard the expression "It wasn't what you said; it's what you didn't say." My father could be very direct, but he could also be very indirect. He never once said that he wanted me to take over the family hearing aid business. Yet whenever I had an opportunity to move out of the area, for example, he would not be in favor of it. The metamessage was that I'd carry on the tradition of fitting hearing aids. I felt like George Bailey in *It's a Wonderful Life*. After my father passed away, I sold the business because I realized that, while it worked for him, it didn't work for me.

ONE-UPMANSHIP VS. EQUALITY

Men are either one up or one down in their relations with others. One winter day when the power went out in the neighborhood due to a snow storm, I decided that I'd go outside and shovel rather than sit around in the dark with no heat. I was out shoveling and a neighbor, who was new to the neighborhood, walked down his driveway. Neighbors who don't normally talk to each other all of a sudden become best friends during a storm or other crisis. Anyway, we got talking about the situation. He had his shovel in his garage, which he couldn't open because it was operated by electricity. When he told me this, I mentioned that I had an extra shovel if he wanted to use it (my garage door was manually operated). He said he did, so I lent it to him to use. I was glad I was able to help him out. But I must admit that I felt one up on this neighbor who rarely even said "Hello" to me. (After that we got along fine).

Control often gets in the way of communication. One person feels superior to another, either because of class, age, gender or race, and this affects the tenor of conversations. Haughtiness is a huge barrier to effective communication.

We express things extremely differently on paper vs. over the phone or in person. Voice inflections and vocal variety can mean the difference between acquittal and incarceration when you say, for example, "I shot the sheriff." That's why

Linguistics

it's important to be careful when you're being quoted in the press. What if you really said, "I shot the sheriff?" Some people have trouble with punctuation regarding quotations. Sometimes it goes inside the quotes and sometimes it goes outside. This small matter makes a huge difference. Using the previous example, do you notice the difference if I say "I shot the sheriff"? Another example is "You've got class." Think of how many different ways you can say this. You can accentuate different words, giving the sentence new meaning every time you do. For example Rodney Dangerfield in the movie *Back to School* said "call me sometime when you 'have no class.'"

POWER VS. SOLIDARITY

Once a woman I used to work with was demoted to an inside position, when I was promoted to her job. She got a desk job, and I got the outside sales rep position. While she was training me in the field, whenever we'd enter or leave a building I'd hold the door for her because I was brought up to do so. I immediately realized that she didn't appreciate it, but I didn't know why. Now I do. By opening and holding doors for her, I was framing her as subordinate or inferior—as incapable of doing it herself. She was a liberated woman. This act exacerbated an already difficult situation (the fact that I was taking over her job).

Solicitors (telemarketers in particular) often annoy me by immediately calling me Frank. They might be in their early twenties, and they haven't earned the right to call me Frank. If they want to do business with me, they should know this. This is their attempt to create solidarity and take the power away from me as the potential customer to make a buying decision. On the other hand, I respect people who say "May I call you Frank?" In grade school, I once called my gym teacher by his first name after his colleague did, and he went ballistic. I'll never forget it.

In my work as a corporate trainer, I helped hospital employees communicate more effectively with patients and their family members. Every once in a while, after I encouraged them to err on the conservative side with "Sir" or "Madam" or "Mr." (or "Ms.") Jones, I'd get an employee ask me, in all seriousness, "What about 'Hon' or 'Babe'?" I wanted to retort "You've got to be kidding me!"

FRAMING
Advertisements, to distinguish themselves from content in magazines, often have to say just that ("advertisement") so people will not mistake the ad copy for the magazine's viewpoint. This somewhat cheapens the effect of the ad and its message. When something is wrong in a relationship, couples often say "We need to talk." This frames the conversation as serious in nature and vital to their relationship. Framing basically sets the tone of a communication. In an e-mail message a colon and parentheses :), which is universally recognized as a smiley face, frames the previous sentence as light, as opposed to serious. For example if you read an e-mail message from someone that says you have bad breath and it doesn't have the colon and closed

parentheses (depending on whom it's from), you may want to consider investing in a bottle of Scope or Listerine.

And speaking of Listerine, this product was framed or "positioned" (see the book *Positioning* by Ries and Trout) as seriously medicinal. Starting with its name—insinuating it was named after Joseph Lister, a physician—and tasting like medicine, many people concluded that anything that tastes that bad must kill germs. On commercials, people wearing white coats are perceived as experts (physicians). That is framing.

INTERRUPTING
I remember before I joined Toastmasters, which I thought of as a sort of support group for shy people, I barely spoke up at all. After I joined, I became talkative—almost to the point where you couldn't shut me up. One fellow I met in the organization was a real intellectual. His speech was often slow and deliberate. Sometimes he took a while to get the words out. In my newfound loquaciousness, I would get impatient and put words in his mouth or try to pull the words out of him when he was speaking. This annoyed me (as well as him, no doubt) because I used to speak like he did and would get upset when other people were impatient with me. In my conversational speech I would often search for just the right word. This would result in long pauses—often in the middle of my sentences. I was intent, as I'm now sure he was, on using precise wording to express myself. I now realize that it's probably not as important as I thought it

was to be so stingy with my words. Nevertheless, I felt bad that I had become an interrupter. I had, I later realized, dominated the conversation, instead of letting him say what he really wanted to say.

Right after I graduated from college I was a bit of a mumbler. At that time I had an acquaintance who was dominant in my life who insisted on finishing my sentences. It was humiliating.

I was also shy growing up—silent, even. My sister, on the other hand, was outgoing and uninhibited. I couldn't understand how she could be so effusive. She couldn't understand how I could be so reticent. Even my cousin, who lived with us while attending college nearby and who was ten years older than me, would often flinch at my sister's gregariousness. I remember one occasion after my sister had joined the Navy and moved out to California. She returned for a visit once, and our family went out to dinner. We ran into a high school classmate of mine. My sister unabashedly spoke up (one might even say she yelled) during our brief encounter with him. Although I knew him well and was not really embarrassed by her outburst, her volume startled me, not just because of its reckless abandon, but also because I knew I could never act like that; I could never be that uninhibited in a conversation in a public place. Her intonation was intimidating to me.

Linguistics

APOLOGIZING
I know I have a difficult time apologizing for
things I've done wrong. I usually make up my
mind I'm going to confess to it, then I blurt out
my apology. It is often awkward, not just for me
but for both parties. To me, apologizing is one of
the hardest things to do in conversation.
Admitting you were wrong is bad enough, but you
really have to acquiesce and give all your power to
the other person, at least for the moment, if not
longer. I have a hard time with it. I'm sure it's a
control thing.

I guess from a man's point of view, apologizing
goes against my nature. It puts me in a one-down
position, which men resist. It makes us feel
incompetent and less effective. Yet apologizing
can be enormously helpful. Studies have
indicated that if doctors make a mistake, but
apologize for it, patients are less likely to sue
them.

SHHH!
At a youth gathering I once attended as an adult,
an interesting thing happened. The youth, with all
their adrenaline flowing, were talking amongst
themselves whenever they felt like it. But the
speaker was trying to get them to listen so he
could deliver a message. The first few times he
addressed them, he raised his voice so as to be
heard over the din of their jabbering. I suggested
the next time he was in that situation he just
remain silent. He did and this is what happened:
Everyone was talking and the speaker wanted to
speak, so he said something to get their attention.

Men Really DO Listen

A number of them, listened but others continued to talk. The speaker remained silent. What happened next was amazing. He continued to remain silent for about five to ten seconds. Those who wanted to hear the message started shushing the ones who were talking. By remaining silent, he got several of them on his side. This snowballed to the point where he got them all on his side, and he was able, once and for all, to deliver a message without any distractions.

I knew it worked, but I wasn't sure why. Now I know why. It had to do with peer pressure, which is huge in the world of youth. Another thing he could have done—if a few people still wouldn't stop talking—was walk over toward them. If they continued to talk, he could ask them if they had something they wanted to share with the entire group. It would have put them on the spot, and unless they came up with something profound or extremely creative, they would have been reduced to their proper place, as part of a group, rather than as the leader. The peer pressure on them at the time would've been tremendous, and if they didn't come through, they could learn a lesson they wouldn't soon forget. Once you know what motivates people, you can persuade them, sometimes with complete silence. It's amazing that you can get people to do what you want just by being quiet!

I'm intrigued by how we try to talk things out in this country. If our communication isn't working, we want to talk about it. Well, isn't talking what caused the problem in the first place? There's an old expression: "If you want to get out of a hole, stop digging."

KINDS OF QUESTIONS
Salespeople know quite well the difference between open-ended and closed-ended questions. They often start a dialogue with open-ended questions to gather information about the prospect. Only after they uncover needs, do they start making suggestions or switch to closed-ended questions.

An example might occur in a car dealership. If the salesperson doesn't know the prospect (which, amazingly enough, is often the case. Why don't they go after repeat business anyway?), they might start with "How can I help you?" or "What are you looking for?" or any other question that might get the buyer to put their cards on the table. Only after they've asked a few open "probes" do they move on to closed probes, such as "Do you have a trade-in?" or "Are you looking to buy or lease?" Meanwhile, they've established some rapport with the prospect by allowing that person to speak. Most people like to talk (especially about themselves) and are often less interested in listening.

Couples can learn a great deal from this because conversation and communication are all about give and take. In many ways, it's like playing tennis or ping-pong. One person hits the ball across the net into the others' court, and the other person returns it. The volley continues, and we get enjoyment out of it. In fact, it's said (at least in ping-pong) that you're often playing personality. That means you play up to the level of your competition. If the other person wants to talk while playing table tennis, that's often what you'll do.

The gender difference is that women generally want the ping-pong game (or the conversation) to go on all day, whereas men often want to "win" and get it over with.

It's Not the Words

Thales, the first philosopher, once said "It is not the many words which have the most meaning." Sentences can be delivered in a variety of ways, and women can often tell (much more easily than men) what people really mean when they speak. Therefore, people have to be careful about the way they say things as well as what they say.

In conversational styles, men and women differ significantly. The next chapter deals with the humor that abounds regarding males and females.

"Many husbands want sex in the morning; many wives want sex in ... June." – John Ortberg

Chapter Four

A Source of Humor

Rob Becker has made a nice living off the misunderstandings between men and women. His one-person show, *Defending the Caveman*, has been shown in thirty countries in fifteen different languages. It made history as the longest running one-man show on Broadway. Becker used to do stand-up comedy in the San Francisco Bay area. In comedy clubs, he'd talk about the differences between men and women at great length, and people would say, "That's not stand-up comedy. You have to change the subject." So he turned it into a traveling road show. He no longer performs, but he's hired individuals to deliver the material he wrote over a three year period after he studied anthropology, sociology, mythology and psychology. Becker explains the play as showing that "men have emotions, but they express them differently." As a testament to the validity of Becker's play, Anna Beth Benningfield, President Emeritus of the American Association of Marriage and Family Therapists, said "When I saw

Men Really DO Listen

Defending the Caveman, I knew I had a new homework assignment for my couples in therapy." He basically says men, hunters, are content to do things together and not talk too much about it. They just like to hang out. On the other hand, women, gatherers, like to, well, gather things (like personal information, shoes and purses). He once said something to the effect that when a guy says to his date at the end of the evening, "I'll call you," she thinks he means as soon as he gets home. He thinks he means "before I die."

Becker talks about how baseball is a great sport for guys. You're out there together (but not too close to each other) focused on a goal. You get to nod and spit without saying much. If you let a woman on the field, it's always in the outfield. They collect in the middle and start talking!

Men are hunters. Women are gatherers. Men can only do one thing at a time. That's the way we evolved. As Becker says, "Men don't watch TV, they actually become the TV." When a woman is talking while a man is watching TV, a man perceives that as external noise. He doesn't want any part of it. It sounds like a buzzing noise, and it's getting louder and louder. A man often wants to use the remote control to turn this external buzzing noise down—or off.

He says a man speaks 2,000 words a day and a woman 7,000. A man comes home from work having used up all his words, and his wife is just getting started! Shakespeare might say of the man (as Horatio said to Hamlet in their exchange

A Source of Humor

with Osric), "His purse is empty already. All his golden words are spent."

Men prefer tool talk, while women talk about people. One segment talks about how men bond by showing each other their latest tools. The television show *Home Improvement* was popular while *Caveman* was in its embryonic stages.

Men don't get the details women get at gatherings. The show doesn't take sides. Kevin Burke, an ordained minister who delivers the material regularly in Las Vegas, married a couple after a performance in February 2009. Tim Plewman has even written a book about the show.

Laughter is the best medicine. Sometimes men can only laugh at how emotional women are. Gender jokes abound on the internet and elsewhere. The following are some of my favorites related to communication:

There are two times when a man doesn't understand a woman: before marriage and after.

A plane was in flight when the pilot announced it was going down. A woman in first class yelled out, "I need a man to make me feel like a woman." A guy from the back of the plane ran up to the front of the plane, ripped his shirt off and handed it to the woman, saying "Here... iron this."

A man and woman were driving down the street. After a while the man, who was driving, noticed a police car in his rear view mirror. The man

Men Really DO Listen

stopped and the policeman said to him, "Your wife fell out of the car a mile back." And the man replied "Thank goodness. I thought I was going deaf!"

A male therapy client once said to his therapist, "I'm going to refer my mom to that twelve-step group for people who talk too much. On and on, anon."

The son walks down the steps and says to his father, "Twenty." His father replies, "Ten." The son says, "Midnight." His father answers, "Eleven." The father says, "All the usual precautions." And the son says, "Okay." The father then hands his son the keys to the family car and his wife says to him, "You and your son need to learn how to communicate." To which the father replies, "We communicate just fine."

Here's a picture of a woman's brain as compared to a man's brain:

A Source of Humor

THE MALE BRAIN

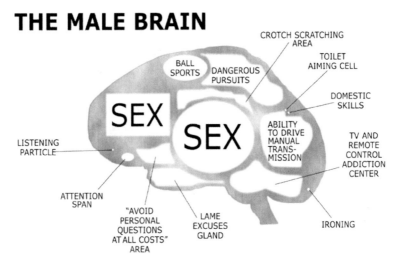

CROTCH SCRATCHING AREA

TOILET AIMING CELL

BALL SPORTS

DANGEROUS PURSUITS

DOMESTIC SKILLS

SEX

SEX

ABILITY TO DRIVE MANUAL TRANS-MISSION

TV AND REMOTE CONTROL ADDICTION CENTER

LISTENING PARTICLE

ATTENTION SPAN

"AVOID PERSONAL QUESTIONS AT ALL COSTS" AREA

LAME EXCUSES GLAND

IRONING

FOOTNOTE: The "Listening to children cry in the middle of the night" gland is not shown due to its small and underdeveloped nature. Best viewed under a microscope.

THE FEMALE BRAIN

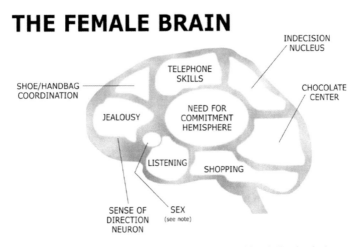

INDECISION NUCLEUS

TELEPHONE SKILLS

SHOE/HANDBAG COORDINATION

CHOCOLATE CENTER

JEALOUSY

NEED FOR COMMITMENT HEMISPHERE

LISTENING

SHOPPING

SENSE OF DIRECTION NEURON

SEX (see note)

FOOTNOTE: Note how closely connected the female sex cell is to the listening gland.

Image obtained via www.twitter-poetry.blogspot.com

Men Really DO Listen

I certainly don't want to foster an Us vs. Them philosophy. Telling gender-based jokes should be more about building bridges than constant warfare. Many studies over the last forty years have all seemed to say that women are good and men are bad. In the 1970s, we were told that men and women are equal. Equality aside, we're different! That's the reality. Get over it.

Section Two

A Few Good Men

Inscape Publishing, a company based in Minneapolis, Minnesota, creates a number of different assessments. The most commonly known one is called DiSC®. It helps people understand their communication style, as well as the styles of others. (Disclosure: I'm a distributor of their products.) In addition to DiSC®, Inscape produces one on time mastery, one on teamwork (called Team Dimensions) and one on listening.

I've had many people take the one on listening, called the Personal Listening Profile®. It generally takes about 15-20 minutes and can be taken on one's computer. After taking the assessment, a fairly elaborate description of the participant's listening style and habits are spelled out. Most people find it to be accurate.

The profile breaks listening down into five different approaches: Appreciative, Empathic, Comprehensive, Discerning and Evaluative. In the chapters that follow, I'll profile some men whose scores were high in each respective category, and in some cases, several categories.

To find out more about Inscape, you can visit their Web site at www.inscapepublishing.com or call 1-800-395-0957.

"You talkin' to me?" – Robert De Niro, in the movie "Taxi Driver"

Chapter Five

Appreciative Listening

The appreciative listener wants to enjoy the listening experience. They like to be entertained and are more likely to pay attention to others if they enjoy their presentation. They listen for inspiration and prefer listening to speakers who make them feel good about themselves, which helps them relax. They also are more concerned about the overall impression the speaker gives than they are about the details being presented.

They respond visibly to color, sound, language and rhythm. They often match the speaker's enthusiasm or playfulness and relax with an open laidback posture. They sometimes encourage the speaker to elaborate on stories.

Pedro

Pedro is a young man in his twenties, who works as a petroleum accountant for a natural gas and oil company. He's single (or as he puts it, "not married yet") and has a girlfriend.

Men Really DO Listen

He predominantly uses an appreciative listening approach. His motivation is often to relax and enjoy the listening experiences he finds himself in. He likes to be entertained, inspired and humored by people.

Perhaps because of his preferred style, he enjoys attending lectures and seminars and even does some presenting himself. As for whether his girlfriend thinks he's a good listener, he suspects that, in her estimation, he's "probably not as good as what I think."

He describes a good listener as "someone who is able to understand what the conveyor is trying to say." Pedro recalls some times when he felt he wasn't being listened to. For example, "when I was with one of my roommates, and I'd be talking to them, and they'd be texting or talking on their cell phone" (when he wished they would listen to him).

In his approach to listening, he pays attention to the context and style of the presenter while trying to find humor in the message. "I can definitely tell you, whenever the person's a real well-spoken individual and they include humor in their speeches, I will be a 150 percent better listener than if they're giving a talk that's really dragging or dull. Keeping communication fun is the key for me," he says.

"Usually whenever I listen to somebody," he continues, "I try to pause for a couple of seconds to really think about what they've said before I start talking." He's comfortable with silence but "not to the point where it's awkward or anything." He tries to slow things down when he's communicating with people.

Challenges

I asked Pedro about his biggest listening challenges. He said, "When I'm with my girlfriend, she would say if I'm watching television and I'm really into a show, I can just phase her out." "Being aware of everything that's going on around me while I'm paying attention to one thing" is a huge challenge for him. He elaborates on the challenge by defining it as "being able to shift my focus to listen to everybody and everything."

Pedro thinks the reason women think men don't listen is because "what we are focused on isn't necessarily the same thing that women are focused on. And because we're not focused on the same thing, they don't think we're listening." He confesses that "sometimes I'm being a good listener to the TV show I'm watching, but not to her." Regarding advice for men who are accused of not listening, he suggests "keeping the volume on the television a bit lower and paying more attention to your significant other."

Sometimes when Pedro doesn't completely understand the situation, he cracks jokes about it. This is his way of dealing with a situation he can't control. Also, although it's a feeling-oriented approach, it doesn't always win him points with his girlfriend, who thinks he's cynical.

Men Really DO Listen

Because Pedro likes to relax while listening, he sometimes misses details. Therefore, Pedro would do well to keep his mouth shut when the topic of conversation is over his head. Pedro needs to learn to use a different approach when the situation dictates it. He would do better to choose a listening approach that considers not only his motivation but also the motivation of the speaker. He needs to be a little more flexible in his listening and determine whether to focus on the information presented, on the feelings expressed or on a combination of the two.

(Turn to page 67 to view Pedro's Listening Profile).

I interviewed Pedro's girlfriend, Collette, after I spoke with him. I started my conversation out by asking her if she thought Pedro was a good listener. She told me she's known him "probably for six years," and she's always been impressed with his listening skills. "That's one of the things that attracted me to him," she said. "He remembers the small things. Someone who's a good listener is very intuitive to everything you say, not just the important stuff. Even when we weren't dating, he was always a good listener. He always seems to surprise me with the things he's remembered that I've said" and [I think] "a good listener is someone who remembers the small things."

We then got into some of Pedro's challenges. "He's so positive that he gets very excited," she said. "He's very supportive, and he's a helping person," but, as a result, "instead of taking it all in...he sometimes interrupts." However, "once you get his attention, he's a very good listener."

When I asked her why men are often accused of being poor listeners, she seemed a bit startled, then said, "The thing I've heard the most is that they're selective listeners." When I told her many people believe that men aren't good listeners, she said, "I've heard that...mostly from my mother." She went on, "A lot of stuff that women or people tend to talk about, they (men) just can't really relate to sometimes. Therefore, they kind of tune out. I see that in myself sometimes: I don't want to hear it. I don't want to listen."

Collette noted that sometimes "there are too many negative things going on. [Men] tend to tune out of negative things. Because I don't think guys tend to be negative. They always tend to be on the positive side. So I think it just depends. But I wouldn't classify them as bad listeners. But, by other people, they do tend to get a bad rap."

She also offered her advice for a man accused of being a poor listener: "Confront that person that thinks that. Have them lay it out for them. Ask 'Why do you think so?' or 'Can you give me an example of a circumstance when I wasn't listening?'"

She and Pedro have many friends who have gotten married, and she believes they "got married too young or they're just having major problems and they've been faced with counseling. One of their issues is listening. When they come home from work, they don't want to hear about each others' stresses. If that's the case, then 'What do you talk about?'"

She recommended that "bad listeners" be more proactive about the issue. "Ask people, 'Why am I not a good listener?' If I felt like Pedro was really ignoring me and it was getting me frustrated, I would just say 'This is something that I feel is important to me and these are the reasons they're important to me." She added, "even if he doesn't know where I'm coming from. I know he doesn't understand my line of work and vice versa, but he sits there and he listens and he lets me get things off my chest. And I do the same for him. ... I think it has a lot to do with eye contact, too. The person may not be listening, but if they're looking at me, they've got me fooled."

If multiple people have accused someone of not listening, she recommends going to all of the accusers individually and saying, "I really want to work on this because I think it's very important, not only in my personal relationships, but with every person I come in contact with."

She continued, "I think everyone has a different definition of what listening is. I feel like I know a lot of women who are worse listeners than guys are. Pedro's definitely 'intuitive.' I think it makes a big difference. You have to have that person define what they think a good listener is or what listening entails. Like I said, it's different for everyone and that can be a big roadblock to a relationship, even if it's a friendship."

Appreciative Listening

Pedro's Listening Profile

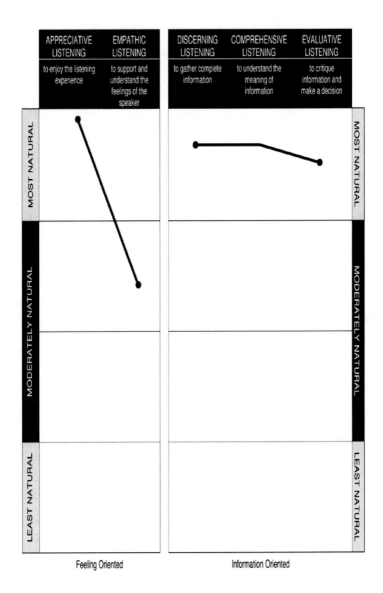

"I like talking about you, you, you, you, usually. But occasionally, I wanna talk about me." – Toby Keith

Chapter Six

Empathic Listening

Empathic listeners are patient listeners. They tend to listen to the feelings and emotions the speaker reveals. They easily relate to a speaker's feelings and may recognize what a speaker wants before the speaker sees it clearly.

Empathic listeners reflect what they hear others saying and let others know that they care about what has been said. As a result, empathic listeners are often approached by people who want to "let off steam." If asked for advice, however, the empathic listener will encourage others to decide for themselves.

People with a preference to empathize while listening want to provide the speaker with a sounding board to offer support and reflection.

Larry

Larry is a director in community theater. His superb listening skills play a huge part in his success. He has helped thousands of people with their budding careers as actors and many friends with their careers outside the theater. He humbly dismisses his talent as "a gift," as if it were given to him, rather than his earning it.

An established actor in his own right, Larry shuns the limelight because he likes to help others. Single and in his early fifties, Larry can be the life of the party as well as a great friend.

Somehow Larry came out high in all the categories of the listening assessment, especially the "feeling-oriented" ones, but his highest score was in the area of empathic listening. If you knew him, you would understand why.

Good actors learn that the other person's "offer" (what they say or do) is more important than what they themselves want to talk about. These days acting is not so much about memorizing lines and saying them articulately, but about complementing the other person (or confronting them, depending on the role). It has as much (or more) to do with chemistry than it does about public speaking. I have seen actors, especially improvisational actors, do some amazing things in conversation that "mere mortals" could not do without years of training.

Larry is a giving person. He'd give you the shirt off his back. He can sing, dance, act, play musical instruments and make you laugh. He's the consummate entertainer. He has many redeeming qualities that are rare in others. Larry is unique

Empathic Listening

and everyone wants him around. He's one of a kind, especially when it comes to listening. He's an outstanding conversationalist, and many people appreciate his listening ability. Larry is undoubtedly a great listener. Women love him, and he has good rapport with men also. He's supportive and amazingly encouraging.

He asks great questions, finds out what the speaker is interested in and talks about that, letting them explore and vent. Other than asking questions, he remains relatively silent, not offering solutions immediately. By allowing his conversational partner to think out loud, he does them a huge favor, and they admire him for it. He accepts their messages without judging, learning from their experiences. In many ways, he's like a counselor or psychiatrist, allowing people to solve their own problems. An ideal sounding board, he permits others' to express their true feelings. As a result, he stays busy in his many pursuits, and people sincerely appreciate his friendship. He has little free time as everybody loves his company.

Larry is the poster child for men who feel they do listen. He listens and he listens well. He also pays the price. Communication, especially listening, is hard work, but Larry personifies the art of listening. While many men wish they could emulate Larry, some of them don't have the communication stamina that he has. Listening can be draining and few people (even women) do it well. Hardly anyone would consider Larry a poor listener.

Men Really DO Listen

Because Larry scored high in all five areas of listening, you might wonder whether he "gamed" the assessment. I can assure you he didn't. He is that good a listener. Probably because of his training in acting, he's able to adapt to the situation and be the best listener possible for the other person in whatever environment he finds himself in.

Challenges

The biggest challenge for Larry is that he rarely talks about himself. He always turns the conversation around to what's going on in the other person's life. As a result, he has a tendency to get tired of other people's dramas.

Another challenge for Larry is that while you would never know that he sometimes struggles in his own life, he does. His ability to mask his feelings can often work against him. Other people are so busy telling him their challenges that his often go unspoken, and therefore, he doesn't get much of a chance to vent. As a result, he often stuffs his own feelings, and they never see the light of day. This habit could potentially be dangerous and unhealthy for Larry as well as those around him.

Besides that, people often dump on Larry. In some ways, he's like the barber who hears everyone's sob stories. After a while, it starts to affect him. Everyone has troubles, but they'd do better if they kept them to themselves. Negative people can be hard to be around. Larry considers

Empathic Listening

himself a people pleaser, and this can be difficult when people don't even believe in themselves.

Larry has other communication challenges, but most are not related to listening. While he gets points for his superb conversational skills, his being an emotional individual can be counterproductive when more rational thinking is called for. Things are a little more subjective for Larry than for many other men.

I didn't get a chance to interview Larry because he's just too busy. He has so many things going on that it can be exhausting just hearing about all that he's up to.

(Turn to page 81 to view Larry's Listening Profile).

After I spoke with Larry, I interviewed Martha, a good friend of his. Here is what she had to say:

"When Larry talks to me, he has a lot of really good eye contact. He's a wonderful actor. In fact, that's one of the reasons he's such a great actor— because he gives you great eye contact when you're on stage with him. So, when you're talking to him, that's obviously something that sucks you into the conversation. It's amazing how many people talk to you and listen to you and don't focus on your face."

"I think Larry has a more female way of listening. Women find that very attractive because obviously men aren't that way. It entails a lot of eye contact, a lot of encouraging statements and not automatically diverting the conversation to themselves. A lot of times—and some women do this, too but not as many women as men—if you're talking about a situation or a challenge you're having or whatever, a lot of times the other person will say 'Oh Gosh, that's just horrible...and it reminds me about what happened to me' and they divert the whole conversation to be about them, as opposed to 'What did you do?' or 'What did you say' and 'What are you going to do next?' and 'How did that make you feel?'"

"By doing this you're really drawing the person out and making them talk out the situation— almost like a therapist. And they end up solving the problem themselves. They're making the decision based on listening to their own version of the story. And they're hearing themselves talk, and their mind is thinking 'Well, maybe this wasn't such a big deal,' or 'Maybe it was a big deal.'"

"Larry has a very engaging way of keeping you focused on the conversation and making sure you're encouraged to open up and share what you would not normally share with other people. A disadvantage to this listening skill is the person you're speaking with might automatically feel they're the most important person in the room. If that person's a female, they may be led into thinking that he's incredibly interested in them— and he may not be. It's always great to be a good listener, but it might possibly lead to a situation where now somebody is calling him all the time because they think there's something there that really isn't there. That probably wouldn't happen so much on a professional level, but if he's at a party and he's talking to a single female and he's giving her all this attention, that could possibly be misconstrued."

"I think Larry really hears you. A lot of people will sit there and be quiet, but he definitely encourages you enough in the conversation with appropriate comments that really let you know that he is hearing what you're saying. He's not just sitting there going 'Uh-huh, uh-huh, uh-huh,' he's making appropriate comments like 'Wow, that would've made me really angry,' or "What do you think you should do next?' so that you're encouraged in the sense that 'This person really cares about me.' There's a level of safety and comfort. He creates a safe environment, which a lot of people don't really have in their relationships, where they can share things that they wouldn't normally share with other people. And I think that makes him a good listener."

She pointed out that Larry was raised by his grandparents, and that generation was one of excellent conversationalists and mostly good listeners—possibly because they didn't have all the distractions we have today. A constant ebb and flow of great conversation occurred when people were sitting around the dining room table that we just don't have nowadays. "That was a different generation," she said.

Men Really DO Listen

Larry has many, many friends. The guy is overwhelmed with Thanksgiving and Christmas invites. Much of that is due to his being a wonderful conversationalist. He can't stand cocktail parties, but he can really work a room if he chooses to. And that's a gift. Martha says, "It really is a gift to be able to immediately connect with someone and have them spilling their guts within about 45 seconds. It's really unique— unless you're a therapist and trained to do that— or a female." She continues, "With men, it's always about them. Somehow the conversation always reverts back to them. 'Oh yeah, I can relate because the same thing happened to me or to a friend of mine.' I think Larry would say that he's a good conversationalist—and I would think he would also say he's shy."

Martha says, "A good listener 'shuts up' and 'doesn't interrupt.' They listen to someone without jumping in. "To be a good listener, you really have to wait for the pauses, wait for the silence—before you step in." Martha, an acting instructor, teaches actors how to play the silences. She says, "A lot of times actors want to fill every minute of every drama or every comedy with a laugh line or a movement or something when it can be very powerful to have a moment where two characters are doing nothing but looking at each other, and there are no words and no movement. I think that's true in life. That's true in conversation. You have to allow for there to be space in conversations for pausing to allow people to feel like they're finished saying what they want to say." Similarly, pastor and author Chuck

Empathic Listening

Swindoll said, "Wise is the person who doesn't feel compelled to fill up the blank spaces.

Martha went on by saying that "it's great when you're talking with someone, and you feel as if you matter—that you're important. I don't think men really view conversation as a way to pass the time. I think conversations for men are a means to an end. Men are often very linear. 'This is point A and I want to get to point C, and you're point B.' So, how fast can I get from point A to point C?"

"Women," she believes, "tend to be more circular. It's more about the conversation itself. That's what's important. Actually, the relationship with that person is what's most important and what's happening in the conversation and the moment of the conversation. Men are often thinking about the next moment. They're kind of thinking 'What do I have to do after point B—which is you—and that's point C."

"That's not necessarily a bad thing," she said. "I think men can be more effective in some professions because they think that way. And I think women can be more effective because of the way they do think, in other professions. It just depends on where you put yourself professionally."

"I don't mean this in a negative way, but men are not as interested in the other person as they are in getting things done. 'What do I have to do to get the sale?' rather than 'What kind of person are you?' 'What's the best way for me to listen to you

or speak to you so you will trust me and like me—
so that we can have a relationship—because
you're going to buy from someone you like,
someone you have a relationship with.'"

If a man is not a good listener and he's told that,
coming up with a constructive way to improve his
listening skills might be in order. They might
want to retrain themselves. Force themselves to
not talk. If they're having a conversation with
someone, they might count to five before replying.
They should probably force their minds to engage
in the process of listening, which, if it comes
naturally to them, is not big deal. But if it doesn't,
they'll have to retrain the brain.

Ways to retrain the brain are to come up with
some good phrases such as "Gosh, tell me more"
or "How did that make you feel?" Open-ended
questions work well. You can retrain yourself to
do that as long as you have an arsenal of phrases
or sentences you can throw in any kind of
situation to help create the conversation.

There's Always Room for Improvement
Martha said, "On a scale from 1-10, Larry's
probably a 9.5." So he has room for improvement.
She continued, "I don't think you can ever say
you've arrived as far as conversing and listening,
which are kind of one and the same. A lot of
conversing goes on when you're listening to what
other people are saying. It's not just about when
you open your mouth and talk."

Empathic Listening

"The good news," Martha declared, "is that if you're not a good listener—and you recognize that and can accept it—you can become a really good listener. It's definitely fixable, whereas a lot of things in personalities are hard to fix. Listening is the kind of thing that can be fixed."

"A lot of marriages fall apart because there's no communication. There's often one person going 'blah, blah, blah,' and the other person's hearing 'La, la, la.' So, there's what you're saying and what the other person is hearing, and they can be two totally different things."

She began to wrap up by saying, "Nowadays, people don't often talk about literature and art and philosophy and spiritual matters. It's more about boring, superficial stuff like—well, I don't want to say the weather, but you know what I'm saying. It's more 'What did you do last weekend?' Back in Larry's grandparents' day, there was no television, no phone, no internet."

One more thing
Martha was loquacious, and I appreciated it. She finished with the following: "One thing you could tell men who are really bad listeners is to go on a silent retreat. Because even if they're not spiritual, one of the challenges that men and women across the board have is finding silence in their lives and using that to an advantage. Whether it's spiritual, or whether it's getting more centered, or whether it's prioritizing or working through a problem you might have, I think we're just bombarded with sound and distractions. So I

think telling people to go on a 24-hour fast of media and sound and the phone ringing would be helpful in this area."

I had a thought afterwards. Perhaps when the earth was being created, in addition to the command "Let there be light," the Lord might've also said, "Let there be silence, at least occasionally."

Empathic Listening

Larry's Listening Profile

APPRECIATIVE LISTENING	EMPATHIC LISTENING		DISCERNING LISTENING	COMPREHENSIVE LISTENING	EVALUATIVE LISTENING
to enjoy the listening experience	to support and understand the feelings of the speaker		to gather complete information	to understand the meaning of information	to critique information and make a decision

MOST NATURAL	●━━━━━━━●		●━━━━━━━━━━━●		**MOST NATURAL**
MODERATELY NATURAL					**MODERATELY NATURAL**
LEAST NATURAL					**LEAST NATURAL**

Feeling Oriented   Information Oriented

"The secret of success is asking the right questions." - Oliver Wendell Holmes

Chapter Seven

Comprehensive Listening

People with a preference to comprehend while listening relate what they hear to what they already know by organizing and summarizing. They're good at recognizing key points and links between one message and another, even when a speaker is disorganized.

Comprehensive listeners listen for how a speaker develops the argument, so they understand its rationale. They may ask questions to clarify a speaker's intention and relate what they hear to their own experience in order to better understand the message. Comprehensive listeners can generally figure out what people intend to say, even if the speaker is not explicit. They can also recognize when someone is saying one thing and meaning something else. Comprehensive listeners can tell when an individual does not understand what has been said, and they will be able to re-explain it more clearly.

Men Really DO Listen

Michael

Michael is an entrepreneur in his seventies, who owns a mechanical device manufacturing company. He's well regarded in his industry as being a good negotiator. He's known in company labor relations and other interpersonal communications in the plant as a good listener.

He defines a good listener as follows: (1) "You don't talk a whole lot, and (2) you ask questions designed to bring the other person's point of view and problem out into the open."
In addition to being a good listener, he also considers himself a problem solver. He said, "The first thing to do in problem solving is define the problem." In the plant, he says, "We're often trying to get to the root of what in the heck was the problem."

Michael knows questions are an important part of listening. He said about questioning, "There are questioning methods that draw people out." He commented that he'd recently read that Benjamin Franklin was extremely effective politically because he spent much of his time questioning, and when he did give opinions, it appeared to be not so much a dogmatic statement, as in "this is the way it is," but he often used the expression, "It seems to me..." Michael said, "I've been trying to adapt that in my own style and I find that it works very well."

Michael had recently been through a long, hard negotiation period. He said, "In negotiating, you're trying to listen, first of all, to what the agenda is, and secondly, to what things are 'give ups,' and what things are hard rock things that are never going to move."

In the hard-nosed business world, salespeople have learned that a Socratic method is much better than trying to ram a product down the throat of a prospect. People would rather feel that they've bought something than that they've been sold something. Question-based selling works much more effectively because questions are less threatening than statements, and the prospects feel they have much more say in the matter.

Comprehensive Listeners
Michael uses what some describe as a comprehensive listening approach. He often elaborates on what his conversational partner has said . His focus is to organize and make sense of information. Relating messages to his own personal experience, he tries to understand the relationships among the ideas exchanged. He likes to determine the rationale of the speaker's argument and listen for the main and supporting ideas presented to him.

Michael can often tell when the person he's speaking with doesn't understand what's been said, and he's able to re-explain it more clearly. Having attended a well-known university, he knows a thing or two about rhetoric, listening for how a speaker develops their arguments, so he can decide whether it makes sense logically.

Men Really DO Listen

He summarizes the information and puts it in the context of his own life. He said, "As a supervisor coming up the career ladder, I was blessed with good problem-solving people and good cost-reduction people. Learning to listen to their ideas and encouraging them was a great help to me."

When asked what recommendations he had for men who were often accused of being poor listeners, he said, "I think you have to put into context what you're listening to and what the purpose of the listening is. It really comes down to a healthy respect for the ideas of others. There is often a kernel of relativity hiding in there."

Challenges

When I asked him if his wife (Michael and his wife have been married over fifty years) considered him a good listener, he replied, "Probably not." The reason he gave was basically that he is oriented toward problem solving and fact gathering. He thinks a high proportion of other talk is feeling and emotion discussion, which is not oriented toward progress on the problem at hand.

He said because he's problem oriented in his listening, his wife thinks he tunes her out if he's not really interested in the social end of things. He admits, "Often I am not really interested, that's all." He says, "If you're problem oriented, that's one set of skills. If you're trying to be empathetic toward someone who just lost a loved one, that's something else entirely."

Comprehensive Listening

When I asked Michael why men are often perceived as poor listeners, he half-jokingly said they have "too much testosterone, and they try to dominate everything." Michael feels men are problem solvers. As a business owner, he likes to see tangible results. Men often think along those lines.

In my discussion with him, he confessed that "I used to dive in when talking to people because I knew where they were going, or at least I thought I did. And that's just plain ignorant and impolite." He went on to say, "It's very tempting, particularly if the discussion gets heated." Now he finds that carefully hearing a person out often is far more productive. Interacting with questions and suggestions, particularly in the research and development effort, often yields multiples of what two individuals could accomplish.

Conflict Resolution
This brought to light the D-E-S-C script method of conflict resolution, which I shared with Michael. In this method, D stands for "Describe the behavior or situation." E stands for "Express your feelings around the situation," S stands for "Specify the action you'd like the person to take," and C stands for the "Consequences that result from the person's cooperation (or noncooperation)."

One could use DESC in the following example: A customer is cursing at a company employee. To resolve the issue the employee might say, (D) "You're using foul language, and (E) that is not helping the situation. (S) If you stop cursing, (C) I'll see what I can do to help you.

(See Michael's Listening profile on page 91).

I interviewed Michael's wife, Katherine, after I spoke with Michael. When I asked her whether she thought Michael was a good listener, she confessed, "I never really considered whether he was a good listener or not." (I couldn't help thinking that perhaps that's the secret to their longevity as a couple). "After you've been married for so many years, you really get to know each other well enough that you don't sit down and have these conversations."

While she thinks he considers himself to be a good listener, she described a good listener as "someone that focuses on the person speaking and actually hearing what they say. Lots of times you can do that but actually not hear what they say. I think he tries. I think he feels it's important in business to be listening to what people are saying."

In describing a time when she felt she wasn't heard, she explained, "When I tell him to stop teasing me, and he doesn't stop, he's obviously not listening. He gets more joy [by teasing her]. Maybe he heard me, but if he ignores it, if he keeps it up, it makes me angry."

Regarding Michael's listening challenges, Katherine said, "He's an intelligent person, and I think his mind could be distracted from listening, because he'll take something someone said and go with it somewhere else." She then backed that statement up, possibly so as not to be disagreeable or controversial, by saying, "I don't know that for sure; I know this is a fault I have, and therefore maybe I'm throwing it on him." She elaborated on the original thought, "He would hear something and then get thinking about it and not hear the rest of what you're saying."

As for why men are accused of being poor listeners, her observation was "I think, as opposed to women, men tend to try to leave emotion out of it. So, they may be hearing the words but not the emotion behind it."

If that's the case, she went on, the way men could change the perception that they're a poor listener is to "look for the emotion. Where is that person coming from?"

Katherine explained that she has made an effort to improve her own listening skills, "When my children were in junior high, I was part of the Parent Teacher's Association, and they had a course there called Active Listening, so I took it. (Active listening is to repeat the sense of what the speaker said to you to see if you captured what it was that they were saying). I tried it on both of our children. Unfortunately, with the older, our daughter, Michael happened to be in the room [when I began using it]. They picked up on it right away and began teasing me about it."

Men Really DO Listen

"Boy, it worked like a charm with our son because neither my daughter nor Michael were in the room when I used it. And I think it was very good. Really what it was saying was 'Is this what you mean? This is what I heard.' And they will either agree or disagree with you."

Regarding what men can do to improve their listening skills, she said, "If someone requests something, heed it. By doing what the requestor says, that proves you heard what they said. Don't act like 'I hear you, but I'm not going to pay any attention to you' or 'I'm not going to do what you ask.' Don't just hear it, heed it.'"

Perhaps to be conciliatory, she said words to the effect that it's not always fair to say that. For example, "If I say something is not working right, he, who's very good at fixing things, gets on it."

One of the final things she said in the interview was that "there gets to be a relationship that's kind of taken for granted." After over fifty years, I would imagine so.

Comprehensive Listening

Michael's Listening Profile

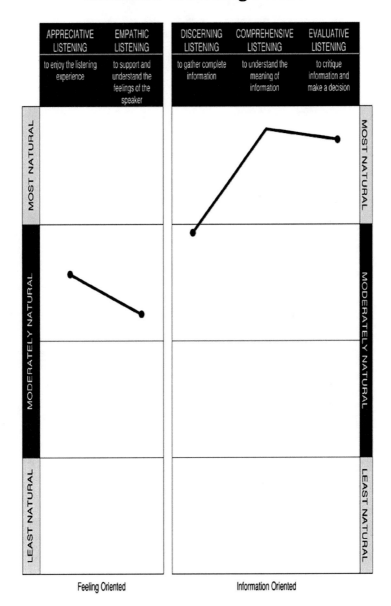

APPRECIATIVE LISTENING	EMPATHIC LISTENING		DISCERNING LISTENING	COMPREHENSIVE LISTENING	EVALUATIVE LISTENING
to enjoy the listening experience	to support and understand the feelings of the speaker		to gather complete information	to understand the meaning of information	to critique information and make a decision

Feeling Oriented   Information Oriented

"Only speak if it improves the silence."Anonymous

Chapter Eight

Discerning Listening

People with a preference to discern while listening want to make sure they get all the information. They frequently take notes on what a speaker says so that they will not forget it. Discerning listeners want to know what the main message is, and they focus closely on any presentation or conversation.

In addition to the message, discerning listeners usually remember the speaker's appearance, behavior, and voice. Discerning listeners find distractions annoying and will do their best to eliminate them. They will likely tune out if too many distractions are present at any time while listening.

Byron

Byron is in his thirties and was engaged to be married when I interviewed him. He's a human resources professional, and his then-fiancé (now his wife) is a physician. He has a master's degree and is an independent consultant. A gifted musician (a classically trained pianist), he's also an author.

Men Really DO Listen

In addition, Byron is a leader in a worldwide learning organization. In that capacity, his ideas and insights are often shared with others, not only orally (in person and over the phone), but also via e-mail. Because his generation prefers the convenience of electronic communication (e-mail) over phone calls, his correspondence often takes that form.

While Byron has exceptional computer and information processing skills, the listening profile indicated that his interpersonal skills could use some improvement. The assessment seemed to be eye opening for him. His scores on the feeling-oriented side were low. Conversely and not unexpectedly, his scores on the information-oriented side were very high. After taking it and surveying the results, he conceded, "My empathic quotient was totally rock bottom."

Discerning Listeners
Byron's highest score was in the discerning listening category. Obviously, the profile struck a nerve in him that I suppose he knew deep down, but he wasn't attuned to. With the document in his hand, he couldn't deny it. He admitted, "The reason this is resonating with me is because it's an information document, and I'm seeing it with my own eyes. It's really hitting home."

During the conversation he said, "People think I'm a robot, especially as a leader of (the organization he belongs to)." Enlightened, he added, "There's a lot of corroborating evidence of the touchy-feeling variety that the real experts,

Discerning Listening

the movers and shakers, adhere to and espouse, and you and I should heed it. A word to the wise—this stuff is important."

When asked if he considers himself a good listener, he hemmed and hawed a little and then said, "Sometimes." Then he said, "How's that for a politically correct answer?"

An appropriate environment for discerning listening is when learning and gathering information. Most likely, because Byron is steeped in the learning and development field, that's his approach. Other positions that would benefit from this style might be journalists, students, statisticians, and investigators.

When asked whether his fiancé would say he's a good listener, he said, "It's something I'm working on." Then, when thinking about his situation, he realized: "She's pretty logical, too, although I'm sure she would score higher in the empathic category."

Byron said he used to consider himself a people person. "It's people I like," he said. "I do enjoy that." For him, the assessment revealed that "I'm way more task-oriented than relationship-oriented."

Challenges
With Byron's then-pending wedding (and marriage), he's going to be put in interpersonal situations where he's never been. If listening could actually be given as a wedding gift, I would

encourage him to put the gift of listening on their registry.

But Byron is already a good listener. He just needs to flex more on the feeling-oriented side when the situation warrants it. I have no doubt that he can be empathetic if the situation is really serious, but the reality is that right now he doesn't "do emotion well." Being goal-oriented (as men generally are), the emotion often gets in the way of his achieving his goals, so men often don't go there unless they absolutely have to.

We're in the information age today. But we're human, too, so we have feelings. Byron confessed that "I think the empathic part is extremely important, especially once you leave the office."

When asked why he thinks men are perceived as poor listeners, he said, "Stubbornness and all the stereotypical things that tend to be true." In response to the question "What advice do you have for men who are accused of being poor listeners?" Byron said, "Take the profile and see visually where you are." He summarized, "If your emotional quadrants are mediocre or low, that's a great area for quick improvement."

While he's thorough in his listening approach, he may find that he's concentrating too much on the message and not the metamessage. While he's gathering information, his wife may wish he'd tap more into how people say what they say, rather than the actual words used.

Discerning Listening

Byron may do well to start leading groups (as well as his pending family) from the heart rather than from the head. An extremely bright person, he runs the risk of alienating those who aren't as intelligent as he is.

Feelings are palpable, whereas information is dry. And, at the end of the day, people don't really care about information. As he matures in his role as a leader and a husband (and eventually a father), he'll ruffle a few feathers. But he'll eventually find a style that works for him, and he'll be a great leader. Until then, he'll make mistakes and learn from them.

I tell him what I tell hospitals I work with: "You can have the most technologically advanced organization in the world, but ultimately success comes down to communication and teamwork." He agrees.

(See page 101 for Byron's Listening Profile).

I interviewed Byron's wife, Erin, (they'd gotten married while I wrote the book) after I spoke with Byron. To the question "Is Byron a good listener?" Erin replied "Yeah, generally." Not exactly a ringing endorsement, but, then again, they had only been married about two months when I posed the question.

As for his listening challenges, she said, "Sometimes I have to ask him to let me finish what I'm saying." To me, that sounded candid. As for whether he considers himself to be a good listener, she said, "I think he considers himself to be a mediocre listener." Byron is a wise man, and after taking the profile, he realized he always has room for improvement.

Erin described a good listener as "someone who lets you finish what you're saying, not necessarily let's you finish rambling—if that's what you're doing—but at least lets you get a couple of formed thoughts out and then asks questions of you that show that they're trying to grasp what you're saying and if they're still interested. Those questions should dig further into what you're saying because that way you know they're still with you."

As far as recommendations to men who are accused of being poor listeners, she said, "Don't jump to conclusions halfway through a sentence, when perhaps what will be said in the second half of the sentence will make things clear. So completely hearing somebody is important."

I asked her why men are generally perceived as poor listeners. To this she diplomatically replied, "I don't know if that's necessarily true, but I think that perhaps men are less emotional and women can be more empathetic. That might be part of it. Men can, a lot of times, put emotion aside and get right down to business, to the nitty-gritty, nuts and bolts. And if that's what they're focused on, then I think that can give the effect that they're not listening because they have their mind fixed on what they need to do and what needs to be accomplished. So that might be part of it."

Discerning Listening

"Women, naturally, tend to want to hear emotions and see how the other person's feeling and how whatever they're talking about is affecting them. And I think men don't necessarily do that. Men have good concentration when they're working on something or reading the paper or doing whatever they're doing, and their wife says something like 'Honey, will you take out the trash' or something, and they're so focused that they don't hear."

Other recommendations from Erin for men accused of being poor listeners: "It depends on what aspect it is they're a poor listener in. Is it that they're not hearing motivations of what the other person is saying? If so, look at facial expressions more or tone of voice and body language."

"If it's a problem with their concentration on one thing, and they don't hear what's going on around them. For example, if they're reading the paper and the man doesn't hear his wife or whoever... in that aspect, it's sort of like a filter and only something like 'the house is burning down' will pierce that filter. But other things you're used to, like [if] your wife is always asking you to do something, your mind's going to filter that out." If that the case, then they need to retrain their minds or reset the filter.

When I told her that men sometimes get caught up in semantics, she suggested they "aim for the concept more." For example, if he prefers "Would you take out the trash?" to "Can you take out the trash?" he needs to lighten up. If he argues this point, he probably has more than listening problems to deal with. She says, "Humans are fallible and they may not always craft their sentences in the best way to express what it is they mean to express. But if you're listening to the concept, that'll help you zero in on the meaning of what they're trying to say to you, more so than the wording of what they're actually saying. So maybe it's like a shift of the focus. So, if you can kind of feel out the meaning or feel out the concept of what the person's telling you, that might help someone who's very literal or very hung up on mechanics or structure."

Her advice reminded me of the quote from Cato (the elder), who said, "Know your subject, and the words will come."

Discerning Listening

Byron's Listening Profile

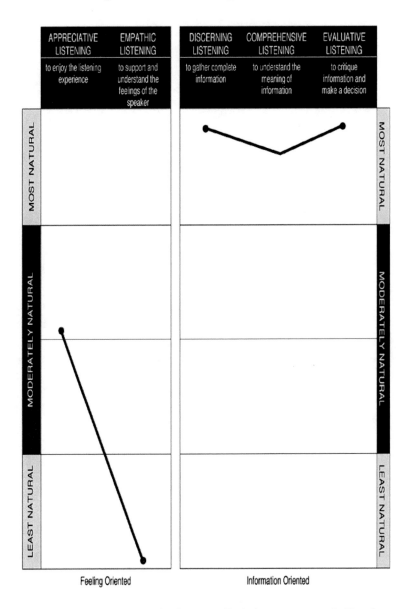

APPRECIATIVE LISTENING	EMPATHIC LISTENING	DISCERNING LISTENING	COMPREHENSIVE LISTENING	EVALUATIVE LISTENING
to enjoy the listening experience	to support and understand the feelings of the speaker	to gather complete information	to understand the meaning of information	to critique information and make a decision

Feeling Oriented   Information Oriented

MOST NATURAL   MODERATELY NATURAL   LEAST NATURAL

"Never miss a good chance to shut up" – Ann Landers

Chapter Nine

Evaluative Listening

People with a preference to evaluate while listening tend to look for the facts that support a speaker's comments. They do not accept something as true just because an expert says it. Evaluative listeners listen for how a speaker develops the arguments in order to critique the message.

Evaluative listeners try to figure out the speaker's intention before responding to the message and may mentally argue with the speaker. They will listen until they know what the speaker is saying, and then they will reply. If evaluative listeners do not like what a speaker is saying, they quit listening. Evaluative listeners also tend to be skeptical of a speaker who is overly enthused about something. They think about how they would present the speaker's message differently.

Tyrone

Tyrone works in a teaching capacity for a company that provides educational services. It's a for-profit company owned by a wealthy businessman.

Men Really DO Listen

Tyrone has been married for eighteen years to an Japanese woman, who speaks English as a second language. Together they have two boys, aged 12 and 8. Tyrone has lived all over the country and has broad travel experiences. He's in his forties.

When asked how he would define a good listener, he said, "It depends on what kind of listener is needed." He went on: "If there's someone that's looking to follow every single detail of something I've told them to do, that person may be an incredible listener. For example, if they can remember, recall, and repeat back to me everything I said, that's impressive. They may even be able to remember the names of everyone in a room they entered for the first time. That's a good listener."

"On the other hand," he said, "There may be a person that couldn't do any of those things, yet they'd be the first person you'd go to if you needed a shoulder to cry on. That's also a good listener."

So listening is not only subjective, it's situational. When I indicate that the listening assessment makes judging a listener a little more objective, he concurs.

As for whether his wife thinks he's a good listener, he said, "It depends on what we're talking about, and it depends on how she's talking. If she's listing off a long list of detailed items and then wants to know at the end of it what she said, or wants me to relist those items, I don't do so well. But if she wants someone that she knows that can sympathize, understand what she's trying to say and bring clarity to it, then I'm a good listener. Otherwise," he admitted, "I seem like an absent-minded professor."

Evaluative Listeners

About the assessment, Tyrone said, "I think it pegged me pretty well."

Tyrone is an evaluative listener. He filters things through his "B.S. meter" and finds many people full of it. His wife sometimes wishes he wasn't so skeptical and instead was more trusting of people. Yet he feels he knows how the world works and, as a result, often questions the sender's motives. He's been in sales and he thinks he knows how many, if not most, salespeople operate (from a "caveat emptor" perspective he says). He knows he's judgmental and wouldn't want it any other way. He realizes that some people might even go so far as to say he's paranoid, but he can rationalize this by telling himself that paranoia is simply "heightened awareness." He insists he's nobody's fool. In reality, he's probably been burned a few times, and therefore he has his antennae up.

Often when he's listening to someone speak, Tyrone is actively agreeing or disagreeing. People often use this style of listening when making a decision, voting, or drawing conclusions. Tyrone uses it often in his world. He's suspicious of other peoples' motives and doesn't always give people the benefit of the doubt, even when they deserve it. In many ways, Tyrone listens as if people are "guilty until proven innocent."

Challenges

Because Tyrone uses an approach that is more judgmental than the others, he has to be careful. During our discussion, he told me about a conversation that went wrong. It was a recent interaction he had at work. "I responded to a situation the way I thought it needed to be dealt with, and I was *completely* wrong because I wasn't really hearing what the situation was. It gave me time to reflect, and I went back to the person, and I admitted that I completely blew it. The approach I followed up with was 'Let me tell you what I think you were trying to tell me—that I didn't hear.' It was a good learning experience for everyone involved," he humbly admitted.

He went on to say, "Listening is oftentimes the ingredient in communication that we fail to understand as well as we should because when we think of communication, we think of the person who is the communicator, and we think the burden of communication resides on them and not the listener. We forget that it's a two-way street."

He then said, "If you get into an argument with your spouse, instead of saying 'You said,' a better thing to say is 'I heard.' This is the case because listening goes far beyond verbal and includes body language and tone of voice."

Evaluative Listening

He's well aware that men tend to be more "fix-it" intended. They're listening to find out "How do I need to respond to this?' or "What needs to be done in order to respond to this?" With his wife, he says, oftentimes she already knows the answers. Rather than giving her his confirmation or approval, she just wants him to simply listen and know she's being heard.

(See page 111 for Tyrone's Listening Profile).

I interviewed Tyrone's wife, Keiko, after my interview with him. When I asked her whether she thought Tyrone was a good listener, she said, "It depends on the definition of a good listener. Yes and no. Yes, when I feel the need of a deep conversation or something important. In that case, I'll say 'Tyrone, I need to talk to you' or 'I need you to listen to me.' At those times, he is excellent. But, in day-to-day conversations, he admits, when I say something and he thinks he heard it right, our miscommunication happens a lot in that setting. It could be the same way for me, too. I have to make an effort. I think both of us have to make an effort to say 'Okay, we need to talk.' We do that often."

As to whether she thinks other people consider Tyrone a good listener, she said, "Yes, I think so. When he's out there, especially at work, he has to be a good listener to do his job well. And I think he's very aware of that. So I believe so [but] I'm just comparing him to other men."

Men Really DO Listen

Keiko says a good listener "focuses on the person who's speaking. A good listener tries to understand what that person is saying. We do have our miscommunications. Part of it is because I'm not an American, and English is not my mother language. So I think it's easier for us to have miscommunication."

Tyrone's challenges in Keiko's view are that "his mind is filled with many things. I think when somebody's talking to you, you have to shut off what's going on in your head and give them your undivided attention. It's challenging for anyone."

As to why men are perceived as poor listeners, Keiko said, "Sometimes women talk too much. We don't get to important points right away. We describe things because we enjoy talking. It's our nature. I'm not saying [this about all women] but most of us love to talk and describe and take time. And maybe men have the attention they need in the first thirty seconds and then they shut off after hearing too many words."

Her recommendations for men accused of being poor listeners are to "initiate the talk with whomever it is [he] needs to talk with, instead of waiting." In the husband-wife situation, "instead of waiting for the wife to explode or get upset, once in a while (especially when a little thing happens where the man did something wrong), initiate the talk. It means a lot to women when men do this. Get more involved in the process instead of waiting, letting it go until it gets worse."

Evaluative Listening

Listening at Its Finest

As for a best case scenario of listening at its finest, she said, "I think I've learned to listen myself. Instead of saying 'First listen to me' or 'Pay attention to me,' I've learned that that doesn't work too well. But when I listen to him first, the conversation always flourishes. We often, on Friday nights, or when time permits on the weekend, we have movie night with the boys. After they go to bed, he and I sit and, over a few beers, converse."

"I try to ask him a meaningful question that he would like to hear. I even ask him about struggles at work that he wants to share or he wants to vent. So I have to be a good listener. I need him to be able to tell me his struggles or whatever. When I listen to him well, in return it is easier for him to listen to me. Those times I really enjoy. We just sit in the den and just talk and talk. Both of us are engaging in the conversation. It can last several hours. Those times are wonderful."

In Summary

All these approaches I discussed over the last five chapters are merely preferences and not set in stone. Basically when a message is being communicated, the receivers need to consider both the speaker's motivation as well as their own. Then they need to choose a listening focus or mode and act accordingly.

The reality is there aren't as many bad listeners out there as there are people who are using the wrong listening approach in certain situations.

Men Really DO Listen

You may have realized I interviewed a wide range of men. Pedro is in his twenties, Byron in his thirties, Tyrone in his forties, Larry in his fifties, and Michael "over 60."

Evaluative Listening

Tyrone's Listening Profile

APPRECIATIVE LISTENING	EMPATHIC LISTENING	DISCERNING LISTENING	COMPREHENSIVE LISTENING	EVALUATIVE LISTENING
to enjoy the listening experience	to support and understand the feelings of the speaker	to gather complete information	to understand the meaning of information	to critique information and make a decision

Feeling Oriented   Information Oriented

Section Three

The Myth Is Dispelled

I've gotten comments during the writing of this book that the concept that men listen differently than women is nonsense. In this section I intend to prove my case, once and for all.

"You are a magnet, I am steel." Walter Egan

Chapter 10

Verifiable Proof

In 2001, then University of Indiana neuroradiologist Joseph Lurito, MD, presented a study at the annual Radiological Society of North America (RSNA) meeting, showing functional MRIs of a man's brain vs. a woman's brain. The stimuli were excerpts from John Grisham's book *The Partner*. According to the study, while in the machine and listening to the audio, women used both sides of their brain while men used only the temporal lobe on the left side.

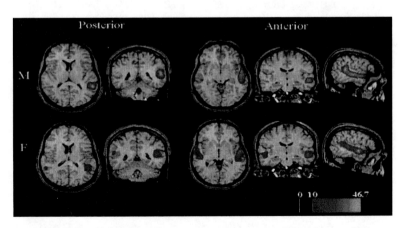

© **Phillips M D, Lowe MJ, Lurito J T, et al. Temporal lobe activation demonstrates sex-based differences during passive listening,** *Radiology* **2001; 220:202-207. Printed with permission.**

Men Really DO Listen

Interestingly, the left side of the brain affects logic, and the right side of the brain is the more emotional side. Creative people are said to be very right-brained.

While I had been presenting similar information prior to Lurito's announcement, this medical study was verifiable proof that men listen differently than women.

Lurito was careful to mention that his finding didn't prove that one gender listens better than the other. In fact, based on his comments he obviously didn't want to start (or should I say rekindle) "the battle of the sexes."

Functional MRIs
The functional Magnetic Resonance Imaging (fMRI) that Lurito used is a noninvasive medical test that measures and diagnoses medical conditions. It maps part of the body (such as the brain) to see where most of the activity is and where it is functioning. It produces multidimensional images of blood flow to various parts of the brain. Functional MRI is used more in research than in clinical areas. It does not use ionizing radiation, or x-rays, so it's less invasive.

Sexual Dimorphism of the Brain
Dr. Jeannette Norden, a neuroscientist and professor in the School of Medicine at Vanderbilt University, says that some of the data from her studies indicate that "at least in some ways, the brains of males and females are different." She professes that "male and female brains can be

distinguished by the basis of how particular structures are organized at gross, cellular and even molecular levels." Her findings reveal that "there are actual structural (and thus likely functional) differences in the way the brain is organized in males and females. While there are no differences in IQ and no significant differences between the sexes in the number of neurons, this doesn't mean that male and female brains don't have different strengths."

The findings show that:
1. Females appear overall to show enhanced language ability and empathy, and the ability to read emotion in other people; they also have superior emotional memory.
2. Males, on the other hand, are clearly superior in spatial ability and in their ability to build systems.
3. In addition to any native differences that might exist, cultures around the world typically exaggerate the differences between males and females.

What she calls sexual dimorphism of the brain, is reflected in:
1. A difference in the size, number, or density of neurons
2. The types of synaptic connections between groups of neurons
3. The expression of particular receptors or other molecules

She indicates that while differences are present among female brains and among male brains, greater differences between male and female brains exist. She indicates that any trained scientist will tell you by looking at a section though particular areas of the brain whether it is male or female. "So we're talking about pretty big differences here," she says.

Male brain pattern, she says, results in an earlier and stricter hemisphere lateralization. In females, however, if the left hemisphere sustains damage, the right hemisphere may take over. This doesn't happen with males. As adults, if a male has a stroke in the left hemisphere, he will have much more trouble recovering than females who have strokes in the same part of their brain. So the strict lateralization works against males in this situation.

Male brains are larger in size than female brains, she states. She also says that even as infants, female children are more attuned to reading faces than males are. In her lecture, she states that the brain's left hemisphere is specialized for language. More males than females have difficulty in schools related to language. They are more susceptible to dyslexia and reading challenges.

She concludes that most neuroscientists would agree that there are differences between males and females: (1) in the body, (2) in the brain, (3) in the mind, and (4) in behavior, although culture, she confesses, has much to do with it. The brain, she explains, is the "biological substrate of the mind."

"Oh Lord, please don't let me be misunderstood."-
Eric Burdon

Chapter Eleven

Men Really DO Listen

The last chapter offered medical proof that men
listen differently than women. Some of you may
still be skeptical. Therefore, I'd like to mention a
few more examples as further proof.

Gray Matter
The latest studies suggest that women actually
have more white matter than men. The
publication *ScienceDaily*, referencing a study at
the University of California, Irvine, says that in
general, "men have 6.5 times the amount of gray
matter related to general intelligence than women,
and women have nearly 10 times the amount of
white matter related to intelligence than men."
Gray matter helps our brains process local
information, like math problems, while white
matter helps us process language more
effectively.

Men Listen with Half Their Brains
I addressed this fact in the previous chapter. Men
listen with the left, or logical, side of their brains.

Men Really DO Listen

This would indicate that they want things presented to them in a logical fashion. If a woman wants a man to remember something, she might want to consider putting it in writing. Conversely, women listen with both the left and right sides of their brain. The right side is the emotional side. This might explain why women are generally more emotional and sensitive than men.

Men listen for facts more than feelings. We've all heard the expression, "It's not what you said but how you said it." This is probably more apt when talking with women than with men. Women listen to metamessages, the message beneath what's said. That's why men are more inclined to talk about history, biography, news, politics, sports, money, business, and how things work. Women, on the other hand, are more inclined to talk about people and relationships. Men also talk primarily to share basic information, but women talk about details. Men are often more direct than women, while women focus on maintaining camaraderie.

Guys are more stoic. They also challenge more and interrupt more. They're also more likely to ignore the comments of the other speakers. In addition, they use more mechanisms for controlling the topic of conversation, including both topic development and the introduction of new topics. On top of that, they use more direct declarations of fact or opinion than do women, including suggestions, opinions, and 'statements of orientation' as Strodbeck and Mann describe them, say Maltz and Borker.

Men Really DO Listen

One downside of men's listening logically is that men normally can't retain a great deal of information when it's presented to them all at once. It's too much. Their minds are on information overload. When this happens, they mentally shut down and say "that's enough." Then they tune out.

Second that Emotion?

Let me share an example of the gender differences in communication: My acquaintance Henry told Alice, his neighbor the realtor, that he wasn't happy with their new neighbors. They'd been in the neighborhood for three months and hadn't mowed their lawn once. Henry called Alice expressing displeasure with the situation. Alice detected a note of accusation in Henry's voice, as if she were to blame, when all she did was sell them the house. Henry dealt with the situation matter-of-factly. Alice, however, got somewhat emotional about it. She saw the situation on the relationship level, the personal level. Henry handled it rather stoically, more impersonally, believing it best handled similarly to how he would deal with the stock market—by taking the emotion out of it. The more impersonal he makes it, the easier it is for him to deal with it. This confirms the commonly held stereotype that men are more interested in the sharing of information where women see conversation on a relationship level. The message is the information conveyed. The metamessage is the relationship, which, after this episode, may be strained. Alice wanted to maintain the camaraderie with the new neighbors. Henry wanted to preserve the value of the neighborhood. Henry comes across on the surface as an ogre, but he doesn't care because he feels that he's doing what, in the long run, keeps the peace in the neighborhood. He fears for the deterioration of the neighborhood because of "one bad apple." His approach and thinking may seem rather cold, but he doesn't care. In his mind, he had better speak up rather than let the neighborhood deteriorate. Alice says "live and let live." Henry is basically saying "get with the program."

In the example above, Henry deals with the situation on an intellectual level, whereas Alice deals with it more on an emotional level. Henry deals with it at the head level. Alice deals with it at the heart level. Henry's argument had more to do with what the Greeks call *logos* (from which the word *logic* is derived). Alice's argument was aligned more with *pathos* (from which the word *pathetic* is derived). Women generally favor indirectness to directness. Alice would never think of talking to the new neighbors about their unkempt lawn. That would be too direct. Henry would prefer the direct approach, thinking it's better to let them know in no uncertain terms how he feels.

Some people might say, "Love your neighbor, not your neighborhood," but Henry sees no reason why the quality of the neighborhood can't be maintained, even if a discussion is necessary. Henry is afraid that if the problem isn't addressed snakes will live in the grass, which he doesn't think is good with children in the neighborhood.

Men Really DO Listen

He thinks if the neighbors let the new couple have their way things will only get worse. He's willing to put his foot down early, so they will think twice about how their behavior affects their neighbors.

The way Henry and Alice see this situation falls along the typical gender lines. Men talk to solve problems, but women often talk to show they're involved with other people. They self-express. With women conversation is more about the relationship than about the information being exchanged.

Men Are More Interested in Independence
In this country, independence is revered, even glorified, among men, whereas women are interested in involvement or intimacy. As humans, we're constantly struggling to balance independence and involvement.

To illustrate this, I once saw a sitcom where a woman was talking to her teenage daughter about the pants the teen was wearing, which were ripped blue jeans. The mother asked her daughter, "Why do you wear those anyway?" Her daughter replied, "They allow me to express my individuality...Besides everyone else wears them."

Men Want to Negotiate
Women are into cooperation. In *Defending the Caveman*, Becker uses an example of a chip bowl running low on chips. If men are sitting around watching television, he says, when the chip bowl becomes empty, men enter into a negotiation about who will get up and fill the bowl. In a group

of five guys, the first one might say, "I bought the chips." The second one might say, "It's my bowl." The third one might say, "I filled it the last time." The fourth one might say, "It's my house." This leaves the fifth guy speechless, so he has to go get up and fill the bowl. This is the way men bond: by negotiating and by being direct.

Nonverbal Communication

Differences in listening and communication don't stop with what men and women actually say. Consider the differences in the following conversational devices.

HEAD NODS

Men nod their heads if and only if they agree with what's being said. Women nod their heads much more often (as if to say "I'm with you. I support you."). One reason for this might be that women like to maintain the camaraderie, while men are looking for credibility in speakers.

POSITIVE MINIMAL RESPONSES

When I was in telephone sales, I used to interject "listening noises" (like "uh-huh" and "mm-hmm") to let the prospect know I was still there and was involved in the communication. I don't believe I do this so much in person as I do over the phone. However, I've noticed that it seems to work by getting the other person to feel comfortable and freer to express themselves more openly. In general, women make more of these listening noises than men. Men, for the most part, remain silent.

Men Really DO Listen

EYE CONTACT
My wife once told me a story about a time when she visited a zoo. A bunch of kids (no doubt boys) were mocking a gorilla. Not surprisingly, he didn't take too kindly to it. After they had their thrill and left the scene, my wife stayed behind and observed the gorilla's behavior. She noticed that he seemed to appreciate that she didn't look him right in the eyes or stare at him.

As boys growing up, we have stare-down contests. We're taught that it's not polite to stare. When boys become men, they often carry that habit (of not looking the other person in the eye) into adulthood. Also, when men do stare, they're often accused of doing it lasciviously (and if a man's eyes roam, he's in trouble).

Over the course of about a month, I spoke with several male acquaintances about various things. One was a lawyer, another a doctor and the third an artist. In all three instances, none of them looked right at me (except occasionally) while conversing. They usually looked off to the side and then would look at me after they'd finished their thought.

Women's Traits
First of all, women have more of a tendency to ask questions. To men, these questions can seem like an interrogation, especially if they don't have the right tone. Now that I'm more aware of gender nuances, I think the tone women use is much better than the tone men use. If a man asks another man a whole bunch of questions, the guy

being asked gets annoyed. When a woman asks the questions, it seems less like an interview with the FBI, unless, of course, the woman is the guy's mother (in which case it can be off-putting).

Secondly, women have more of a tendency to do the dirty work involved in maintaining social interaction. They do more to facilitate the flow of conversation. Usually, men are not as gifted in keeping up with the rhythm of dialogue.

Also, women offer up more positive minimal responses (alluded to earlier). These include "yeah" and "uh-huh," as well as nods. Men nod their heads if, and only if, they agree with what's being said, whereas women nod their heads much more often, as if to say, "I'm with you emotionally. Go on."

When women have been interrupted or receive a delayed minimal response, they are less likely to outwardly protest. Instead, they keep silent. This is less true of men, who often object.

Also, women are more likely to acknowledge the existence of others. They often do this through eye contact. On the other hand, men are more susceptible to looking around the room (or straight ahead). Therefore, men are often more comfortable sitting at a bar, watching sports on TV with a companion, than they are looking directly into someone's eyes. A similar scenario in which men feel comfortable is riding in a car with another person.

Men Really DO Listen

Also, women have a greater tendency to use the pronouns "you" and "we," as opposed to "I," which is used more often by men.

More Men's Traits
Not only are men more likely than women to interrupt, they are also more likely to challenge or dispute ideas. One reason for this could be because men have higher levels of testosterone. I've heard that trial lawyers, in general, have more testosterone than other occupations, even than other attorneys.

Men are also more likely to ignore someone. I once heard a presenter speak on the topic of negotiation. Afterwards, I went up to him to ask him a question. He looked right past me (or was it through me?), preferring to seek out women to talk with. I found it extremely annoying.

Men also have more of a tendency to try to control the topic of conversation. This is probably because they don't want to feel stupid. I suppose it's also because they're less willing to be vulnerable.

Men are either one up or one down in their relationships, especially with other men. Women want to be on a level playing field, not one up or one down. Many people perceive that the listener is in a subordinate position, and men would rather be one up than one down. Many men have listened to lectures from their fathers. They're definitely one down in this position when they are forced to listen. However, men don't mind being put in this position if the information they are being given is interesting. Women are not as interested in receiving information per se, as they are of giving the gift of listening.

Tannen says, "The accusation 'you're not listening' often really means 'You don't understand what I said in the way I meant it' or 'I'm not getting the response I wanted.' Being listened to can become a metaphor for being understood and being valued."

Also, I think men think that by talking, they're displaying their intellect. They often feel less in control when they've been relegated to being the listener.

There's an oft told story of a British woman who had lunch with Prime Ministers Gladstone and Disraeli on separate occasions. Afterwards, she said, "When I had lunch with Gladstone, I felt like he was the most important person in the world. But when I had lunch with Disraeli, I felt like I was the most important person in the world."

The Bottom Line
The reality is that women expect men to listen to them like their girlfriends do (in a more involved, animated way). Men don't. They listen differently. I'm not saying that men aren't as good at listening as women; I'm saying that men DO listen in their own inimitable way.

"If you wish to persuade me, you must think my thoughts, feel my feelings and speak my words."
– Cicero

Chapter Twelve

Suggestions for Better Communication

As I mentioned at the outset of this book, communication is of paramount importance in any relationship. If people can't communicate, it really isn't much of a relationship. Communication between business partners, coworkers and spouses determine whether that relationship survives. It can also mean the difference between surviving and thriving. This final chapter offers some suggestions as to how to communicate more effectively, knowing full well that communication is hard work.

As was previously mentioned, communication has much to do with how we were brought up. In many ways it comes down to our definition of common courtesy. Common courtesy, you might have noticed, is not always all that common. And people have different definitions of what it is. For example, another driver of a car might have a completely different definition of what common courtesy is than I do. Mine happens to include using a turn signal. It also includes not using a handheld cell phone. (Full disclosure: I must confess, at times I have slipped up and not used my turn signal or used my cell phone while driving. And most likely, other drivers have noticed.)

We've all experienced good communication and poor communication. My goal in this book has been to get people to communicate effectively. Therefore, I'll start this chapter by addressing public speaking. Then I'll get into a few more communication items.

Public vs private speaking

As Tannen astutely points out, most books on speaking are about public speaking—while most of the speaking we do is private speaking. The two are very different and only an accomplished speaker can make a public talk seem personal.

Men are more inclined to do what Tannen calls "report" talk (which can include public speaking), whereas women are more likely to use "rapport" talk (usually private speaking). Women want to connect while men often want to show others how intelligent they are.

Public Speaking

One of my favorite sayings about public speaking, attributed to Franklin Delano Roosevelt, is "Be brief. Be sincere. Be seated." Andrew Carnegie expressed it another way: "If you don't strike oil in the first few minutes, stop boring."

Suggestions for Better Communication

From a listening perspective, you must realize that speakers generally speak for one of four reasons: (1) to inform, (2) to entertain, (3) to persuade or (4) to self-express.

In Peggy Noonan's book *Simply Speaking,* she talks about her craft. She was a speechwriter for Ronald Reagan and George Bush. She has also written for many other people. In the chapter entitled "You Have to Find Their Sound," she basically breaks people down into two categories: the linear thinkers and the circular thinkers. She says, "some people have a thinking and speaking style that is logical, linear, point by point. Some are intuitive and make odd but often apt comparisons, sometimes using interesting images. Some people are witty and some are comical and some are neither, or neither very much." A good rule of thumb when writing your own speeches or presentations is to try to find your voice and stick to it.

Communicating over the Telephone

When communicating on the phone, you must take a number of things into consideration. Just because someone answers the phone when you call, doesn't mean they're free (or want) to talk. I've found that a good opening to a telephone conversation is "Did I get you at a bad time?" Often the way the person I'm calling answers that question determines how available (or interested) they are in speaking to me. If I get an answer to the extent that "I have a minute or two," I'll often cut right to the chase without any delay. On the other hand, if I sense they have plenty of time, I won't necessarily get right down to business. Men often exchange facts over the phone. Once their problems get solved, they move on. Rob Becker says his wife's girlfriends call her up just to talk. He said, "If a guy calls me up just to talk, I owe him money."

Sometimes a telephone call to someone can be the best way to communicate with that person. Often this is the case when the person you need to communicate with doesn't do face-to-face conversations very well.

I try to reserve cell phone conversations for emergencies. And I know many people think I'm strange because of this. I'm also aware that many people, particularly young people, no longer have (or use) landlines. Personally, I find cell phones a necessary evil. They're wonderful to have when you really need them, but often a nuisance. Many people talk too loudly when using them and say inappropriate things into them that others often don't care to hear. Users of them often annoy others. As someone once said to me, "Cell phones are the new cigarette."

One of the reasons I don't like them is because of what I call crosstalk. I won't be finished talking, but the person on the other end of the call will think I am and therefore will start talking over me. There are fits and starts. Also, cell phone batteries run low, creating a poor signal. The same is true if the person calling is in a dead zone. All-in-all, I try to use cell phones only as a last resort. I know many people disagree with me on this, but I find cell phones (as opposed to landlines) a poor way to communicate. However, poor communication is sometimes better than no communication.

Body Language
A branch of science called neuro-linguistic programming (NLP) says we can discern whether a person is visually, auditorily or kinesthetically oriented. In theory if you ask a question and they roll their eyes a certain way, you'll be able to know what their tendency is. Then, for example, if they're visually oriented, you might be better able to connect with them by asking them if they "see" what you mean, or if they "get the picture." If they have an auditory orientation, you might ask them, "How does that sound?" Or, you could agree with them by saying "I hear you." If they're kinesthetically oriented, you could ask them how they "feel" about something.

If the person you're communicating with is an intimate partner, a better way to discern their preference is to simply ask them, or to have them close their eyes and describe to you a day at the beach. How they describe it should tell you whether they're visually, auditorily or kinesthetically oriented. Whether they describe sights, sounds or feelings should pinpoint their preferred sense.

A person's vocation (or avocation) can also be a good indicator of a person's preferred communication approach. My wife is a radiologist and is definitely visually oriented. I, on the other hand, used to fit hearing aids, am a sound technician at our church and speak and deliver workshops on the subject of listening. Therefore, my orientation is more of an auditory one. In fact, we live on a busy corner, and often, when I'm out with the dogs in the yard or working there, people will drive by and yell out to me. I can sometimes tell who they are more by their voice than their face.

Hard of Hearing vs. Hearing People

As speakers and communicators, we are sometimes challenged in ways we may not even be aware of. For instance, approximately 33 million Americans have some degree of hearing loss. Therefore, it's quite possible that people you know are among them. You, and even they, may not realize they have this problem. Some of us have family members or other loved ones who are hard of hearing.

There are ways to communicate more effectively with people who have a hearing disability, the most important of which may be not to talk louder—but to talk more slowly. Keep in mind that some hard-of-hearing individuals may not admit that they have the problem.

Helen Keller, who was both deaf and blind, said "Deafness is a worse misfortune, for it means the loss of the most vital stimulus—the sound of the voice which brings language, sets thoughts astir, and keeps us in the intellectual company of man."

Suggestions for Better Communication

Communicating across Genders

Finally, here are a few closing suggestions for women and men to consider as they're communicating across genders:

SUGGESTIONS FOR WOMEN:

1) Find out if the man you're speaking to is an introvert or an extrovert. If he's an introvert, give him space (and come up for air every once in a while, too).
2) If you really want to connect with him, find out what his interests are. If it's football, for example, express an interest in it. Learn a few things about the game. If it is books, find out what he might enjoy reading and buy it for him (if that's appropriate in the particular relationship). The golden rule is "Do unto others as you would have them do unto you." The platinum rule, as defined by Tony Allesandra, is "Do unto others as they would do unto themselves." Your male acquaintance might like to read but might not enjoy fiction (like you do). If that's the case, don't buy him a novel. Perhaps a biography would be more to his liking. Instead, you may want to find out who his heroes are and buy him a book by or about whomever that is.
3) Be direct with him. Confront him. Challenge him.
    a) In the intimate relationship, you might say "I need to vent" or "I have three things I want to tell you" (and then keep it to three).

    b) If you don't want him to solve your problems, tell him, "I just need you to listen to me. Will you do that?"

    c) Use open probes. For example, instead of asking "How was your day?" try "Tell me about your day."

    d) Psychologist Thomas Crook suggests "When you want to have a heart-to-heart conversation with a man, tell him you want him to solve a problem for you. That will appeal to his action-oriented nature."

4) Recognize the innate differences between people, especially between men and women. It's in the chromosomes.

5) Have a sense of humor.

6) Thank men for listening. They often don't understand how important it is to a woman to be listened to, to be heard.

SUGGESTIONS FOR MEN:

1) Here is a radical idea, but it can be fun and educational. It might even appeal to men's competitive nature. With a bunch of people, play a game called "Personal Pronouns." It goes like this: Carry on a conversation with someone without using any personal pronouns. The first person who uses "I," "we" or "me" is eliminated and should sit down. The person left standing finds another partner and carries on a (regular) conversation. The last two people standing carry on a conversation with the others listening.

Suggestions for Better Communication

Several stipulations apply. No speaking in the third person. In one Seinfeld episode, a guy named Jimmy was hitting on Elaine in a gym, saying things like "Jimmy thinks Elaine is attractive." (Bob Dole, I've read, also often spoke in the third person). I think you'll find this a challenging exercise that will help people realize how often we talk about ourselves. Besides, you might learn something.

2) Think about what your partner needs, feels and expects from you.

3) Check your ego at the door. The opening line to Rick Warren's best-selling book, *The Purpose Driven Life* is "It's not about you."

4) When your partner indicates she'd like you to listen to her, ask her if she'd like you to be "the brain" (logical, problem solving) or "the ear" (empathetic).

5) Put the time in. Listening takes time. Think of it as Felsburg's law: If you're doing something you don't often do, allow more time for it than you think is required. For example, if you think something you have to do around the house is only going to take an hour to do, allow three hours. If you think it'll take three hours, allow the whole day for it. That way you're more patient while doing it, and you don't make as many mistakes.

6) Remember, to your spouse listening means intimacy. Spending time is a priority that can't be compromised. Partners are productive when they're happy.

7) Take turns listening and speaking with your partner. Be the listener for 15 minutes while she speaks, then be the speaker for 15 minutes while she listens.

SUGGESTIONS FOR BOTH PARTNERS:
1) Remember, speaking is an audience-centered sport. Make it interactive.
2) Get a copy of *The Five Love Languages* by Gary Chapman. The author discusses how we all respond to different things and, just because I respond to something favorably, that doesn't mean my partner will.
3) Take a DiSC© profile. It will help you understand your communication style and the styles of others. I (and others) have found it life changing. Another option is the Myers-Briggs Type Indicator® (or MBTI). See Appendix A for details.
4) If you can afford it, consider a weekend retreat to get to know your spouse better. Many organizations sponsor them and run excellent workshops (See Appendix B for details). There's nothing like a weekend away to get rejuvenated and to get a different perspective on life.

Conclusion

The reality is that women expect men to listen to them the way other women listen to them—without judgment. Men are brought up to be problem solvers and negotiators. If a woman's talking to a man, she often just wants him to be a sounding board. But a man's tendency is to solve the problem and get it over with. Women would often rather be understood than have their problems solved for them (often because it makes them feel like a patient with a male doctor).

On the other hand, men would rather have their problems solved for them. Women often expect men to listen to them the way they're used to being listened to by other women. Because women grow up in different worlds than men, they are treated differently, talked to differently and talk differently as a result.

Men speak, act and think differently than women, so it's no surprise then that they listen differently. Knowing this helps us communicate more effectively across genders and in "mixed company."

So Long

Instead of saying "Goodbye," I'll echo former Cubs and Saint Louis Cardinals radio announcer Jack Brickhouse, who I'm told used to sign off by saying, "Thanks for listening."

Bibliography

Adler, Mortimer, *How to Speak, How to Listen*

Ailes, Roger, *You Are the Message*

Allesandra, Tony *The Platinum Rule: Discover the Four Basic Business Personalities and How They Can Lead You to Success*

Beck, Aaron T, *Love Is Never Enough*

Becker, Rob, *Defending the Caveman* (Broadway Show)

Burley-Allen, Madelyn, *Listening: The Forgotten Skill*

Cameron, Julia, *The Artist's Way*

Chapman, Gary *The Five Love Languages: The Secret to Love That Lasts*

Covey, Stephen, *Seven Habits of Highly Effective People*

Craine, Michael *Hear Well Again*

Faber, Adele, and Elaine Mazlish, *How to Speak So Children Listen and Listen So Children Speak*

Gray, John, *Men Are from Mars, Women Are from Venus*

Goleman, Daniel, *Emotional Intelligence*

Gordon, Thomas, *Active Listening*

Hendrix, Harville, *Get the Love You Need*

Jung, Rex, Michael T. Alkire, Kevin Head, and Ronald A. Yeo, "Intelligence in Men and Women Is a Gray nd White Matter." *ScienceDaily.* (Jan. 22, 2005) Retrieved August 14, 2010, from http://www.sciencedaily.com /releases/2005/01/050121100142.htm

Kindlon, Dan, and Michael Thompson, *Raising Cain*

Men Really DO Listen

Lakoff, Robin *The Logic of Politeness, or Minding Your P's and Q's*

Lerner, Harriet, *The Dance of Intimacy*

Lever, Janet, "Sex Differences in the Games Children Play." *Social Problems*

Lurito, Joseph, and Michael Philips, "Temporal Lobe Activation Demonstrates Sex-based Differences during Passive Listening." *Radiology* July 2001: 220:202-207

Mackay, Harvey, *Swim with the Sharks without Being Eaten Alive*

Maltz, Daniel N., and Ruth A. Borker, *A Cultural Approach to Male-Female Miscommunication*

McWhorter, John, *The Power of Babel*

McWhorter, John, *Doing Our Own Thing: The Degradation of Language and Music and Why We Should, Like, Care*

Noonan, Peggy, *Simply Speaking*

Norden, Jeannette, *Understanding the Brain*

Nichols, Ralph G., and Leonard A. Stevens, *Are You Listening?*

Peck, M. Scott, *The Road Less Travelled*

Perret, Gene, *Become a Richer Writer*

Pipher, Mary, *Reviving Ophelia*

Ries, Al, and Jack Trout, *Positioning*

Steil, Lyman, and Richard Bommelj, *Listening Leaders*

Tannen, Deborah, *That's Not What I Meant*

Tannen, Deborah, *You Just Don't Understand*

Whiting, Robert, *You Gotta Have Wa*

Wolvin, Andrew D., and Gwynn Coakley, *Listening,* 5th Edition

Appendix

Appendix A

Myers-Briggs Type Indicator® (MBTI)
Published by CPP Inc.
1055 Joaquin Road
2nd Floor
Mountain View, CA 94043
www.cpp.com
650-969-8901
800-624-1765 (Toll Free)
650-969-8606 (Fax)

Inscape Publishing
6465 Wayzata Boulevard
Suite 800
Minneapolis, MN 55426
1-888-575-8800
www.inscapepublishing.com

Appendix B

Family Life
P O Box 7111
Little Rock, AR 72223
800.FL.TODAY (800.358.6329) Outside the US:
501.223.8663
Weekend to Remember
www.weekendtoremember.com

Dr. Howard J. Markman
Love Your Relationship Inc.
1082 Love Court
Denver, CO 80303
303.482.7588
1.866.601.LOVE
303.783.9449 (Fax)
www.loveyourrelationship.com

<u>Men Really DO Listen</u>

Emerson & Sarah Eggerichs
Love & Respect Conference
www.loveandrespect.com
Love & Respect Ministries Inc.
770 Kenmoor Ave SE
Suite 101
Grand Rapids, MI 49546
616.949.9790

<u>Biography</u>

FJ Felsburg has facilitated hundreds of listening workshops and has spoken around the world. A former hearing aid specialist, Felsburg is an Inscape distributor and works in international communications. For further information, email <u>felsburg@comcast.net</u>.

QUICK ORDER FORM

Telephone Orders: Call 484.680.0962. Please have your credit card ready.

E-mail orders: mrdl@CogentTraining.com

Postal Orders: Cogent Training, P O Box 852, Narberth, PA 19072-0852, USA Telephone: 484.680.0962

Please send the following books or CDs. I understand that I may return any of them for a full refund—for any reason, no questions asked.

_____

_____

Please send me more FREE information on:
____ Training   ____ Speaking   ____ Consulting ___ Seminars

Name: _____
Address: _____
City: _____ State : ___ Zip: _____

Telephone: (W) _____ (H) _____ (C) _____

E-mail Address: _____

Sales tax: Please add 6% for products shipped to Pennsylvania addresses.

Shipping by air
U.S.: $4.00 for first book or and $2.00 for each additional product.
International: $9.00 for first book or $5.00 for each additional product (estimate).

Also available from the author for the same price ($20 + S/H) are the CDs *The Art of Effective Listening* and *Telephone Skills.*

Payment: Check   Credit Card: Visa   MC   AMEX
Card Number:_____
Security Number _____ Exp Date: _____
Name on Card: _____